IDENTIFYING

ORCHIDS

The new compact study guide and identifier

ORCHIDS

The new compact study guide and identifier

Rick Imes

CHARTWELL
BOOKS, INC.

A QUINTET BOOK

Published by Chartwell Books
A Division of Book Sales, Inc.
114, Northfield Avenue
Edison, New Jersey 08837

Reprinted 1996

This edition for sale in the U.S.A., its territories
and dependencies only.

ISBN 1-55521-839-3

This book was designed and produced by
Quintet Publishing Limited
6 Blundell Street
London N7 9BH

Creative Director: Richard Dewing
Designer: Nicky Chapman
Project Editor: Stefanie Foster
Editor: Fredericka Stradling

Typeset in Great Britain by
Central Southern Typesetters, Eastbourne
Manufactured in Singapore by J. Film
Printed in Singapore by
Star Standard Industries Pte. Ltd

CONTENTS

· · · · · · · · · · · · · ·

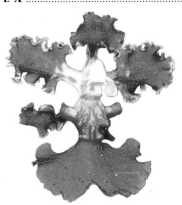

INTRODUCTION

Orchidaceae is the largest family in the plant kingdom, and its members are among the world's most specialized plants. There are more than 30,000 known species, and more are being discovered and documented every year. Though the majority are concentrated in tropical rainforests and cloud forests between 3,000 and 9,000 feet (914 and 2740 metres) in elevation, orchids range from the southern extremities of South America, Africa, Australia, and New Zealand north towards the Arctic Circle, and from lowland plains to alpine treelines. Most are **terrestrial** (rooted in the ground), **epiphytic** (growing nonparasitically above the ground on another plant), or **lithophytic** (growing on the surface of a rock).

ORCHIDS IN CULTIVATION

Orchids are grown essentially for their beautiful and intriguing eye-catching flowers. However, one, the Vanilla orchid *(Vanilla planifolia)*, has economic value as the source of the familiar flavour used in ice-cream and cake recipes around the world. There are also orchids which have long been used by primitive peoples for medicinal purposes. The bulb of an African *Ansellia* species, for example, is chewed and sucked as a remedy for various ailments.

Phalaenopsis schilleriana.

A simple shade house construction.

Mystique has surrounded orchids for centuries, seen in numerous old prints depicting oriental orchids, particularly in China and Japan. The Japanese admired orchids as long ago as the eighth century. They were popular with the rising wealthy merchant class, and the less common varieties were particularly prized by court nobles. These species, selected for their rarity and variety of colour, often cost hundreds of thousands of yen. The first orchid to be recorded in both written and graphic form by the Chinese was *Cymbidium ensifolium*.

The modern hobby of orchid cultivation probably began in the early eighteenth century with the collecting expeditions that were financed by wealthy European enthusiasts. The delicate constitution of most orchids meant that few survived the long voyages back from their country of origin and the survivors were very highly priced as a result. It was not until 1891 that the boom in orchid cultivation began, when the discovery of a huge population of *Cattleya labiata*, combined with a higher survival rate due to faster transit, made these orchids affordable. With the extensive research into orchid reproduction and cultivation, the pleasure of growing these marvellous plants can now be enjoyed by everyone.

Dendrobium speciosum *in its natural habitat.*

HABITAT

In the tropical forests, to which many orchids are native, vegetation is thick and lush, and the competition for light is fierce. Many orchids, in response to this environmental pressure, have evolved into epiphytes. These are plants which grow on other plants, logs, ledges, or other elevated spots where some humus may have accumulated. Epiphytes extract no nutrients from their living hosts, but obtain most of their needs from the bit of decaying organic matter in which they are rooted and from the trace elements in air and rainwater. These "air plants" cannot draw water from the soil as their terrestrial cousins do, and have therefore evolved roots with spongy surfaces that soak up rain, mist, and dew on contact. They have swollen stems, called pseudobulbs, and thick, leathery leaves, both of which aid in conserving water. Epiphytes that are more resistant to desiccation and need lots of light grow higher up on trees, while those less resistant to dry conditions, and more shade tolerant, will be found lower down, often on the same tree. When epiphytes are grown in a pot or hanging basket, a very porous medium must be used to allow air circulation around the roots. Terrestrials, which grow in open forests, meadows, or along streams, require a loose compost rich in humus.

Cattleya bowringiana.

GROWTH PATTERNS

Most orchids have one of two basic growth patterns: **sympodial** and **monopodial**. Sympodial growth, the most common, has many stems, or pseudobulbs, arising from a creeping rhizome, which itself is a modified stem. A new growth, called the lead, originates each year from the base of the pre- ceding year's stem. Generally only the newest pseudobulb produces flowers. Monopodial plants have only one main stem that produces no new growth from the base but adds new leaves at the top. Flowering stems and aerial roots originate between the leaves, and the stem of some species branches from buds in the leaf axils.

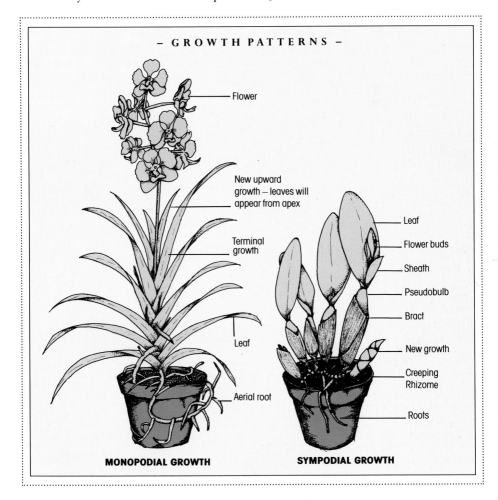

– GROWTH PATTERNS –

Flower

New upward growth – leaves will appear from apex

Terminal growth

Leaf

Aerial root

MONOPODIAL GROWTH

Leaf

Flower buds

Sheath

Pseudobulb

Bract

New growth

Creeping Rhizome

Roots

SYMPODIAL GROWTH

STRUCTURE

Despite the complex appearance of many orchid flowers, they actually have a very simple structure consisting of three outer parts, the sepals, and three inner parts, the petals. The two upper petals are identical, while the lower one, the lip, is modified so that it is usually quite different from the others. The lip often has its own shape, coloration, and ornate crests, ridges, fringes, horns, or other features. Sometimes the lip is greatly reduced in size, but usually it is the most striking part of the flower. The least conspicuous part of the flower, which is often the defining characteristic of a species, is the column, fused reproductive parts located in the centre of the flower. Though unique to each species, all have a pollen-bearing anther, the male part, at the tip, with the female stigma, a receptable filled with sticky fluid, directly below. Pollinating insects are attracted by nectar, and the pellets containing pollen, the pollinia, are attached by a diverse assortment of ingenious methods to the insects as they leave the flower. When the insect visits the next flower of that species, the specialized stigma receives the pollinia. Thus cross-pollination is achieved, ensuring genetic diversity within the species, and allowing it to evolve in keeping with environmental changes. However, a pollinated flower quickly wilts, so pollination is usually avoided by hobbyists unless they are intent on propagating orchids from seed, a very delicate and tedious process.

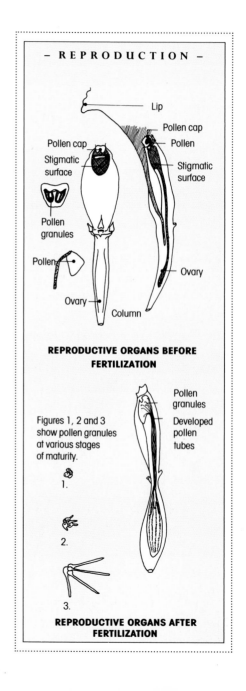

– REPRODUCTION –

Lip
Pollen cap
Pollen cap
Pollen
Stigmatic surface
Stigmatic surface
Pollen granules
Pollen
Ovary
Ovary
Column

REPRODUCTIVE ORGANS BEFORE FERTILIZATION

Figures 1, 2 and 3 show pollen granules at various stages of maturity.

1.

2.

3.

Pollen granules
Developed pollen tubes

REPRODUCTIVE ORGANS AFTER FERTILIZATION

– THE NAMING OF ORCHIDS –

The naming of orchids follows strict conventions, originally laid down by the Royal Horticultural Society in a publication called *The Handbook on Orchid Nomenclature and Registration*. The terms used include:

Family
Orchidaceae

Subfamily
The orchid family, which is huge, is broken down into subfamilies, eg *Cypripedoideae*.

Tribe
Subfamilies, in turn, are broken down into tribes in many cases, eg tribe *Oncidiinae*.

Genus
A group of species that are allied, eg *Paphiopedilum*.

Species
A naturally occurring interbreeding group within the genus, eg *P. callosum*.

Artificial Hybrid
Offspring derived derived from the cross-pollination of two orchids. The name must be registered with the RHS, eg *P.* Maudiae.

Parentage
The maternal or pod parent and the paternal or pollen parent, eg
P. callosum x P. lawrenceanum.

Selected cultivars
Unlike most plants, many orchid groups with hybrid parents are given in roman type without quotation marks, eg *Paphiopedilum* Freckles, which covers a group of hybrid cultivars with similar parentage. Within a group, individuals may be recognized as cultivars, eg *Paphiopedilum* Lyric "Glendora".

Award
Any distinction granted, eg FCC/RHS. The full title of an orchid would therefore be written as, for example, *Paphiopedilum* Maudiae "Magnificum" FCC/RHS
(P. callosum x P. lawrenceanum).

ORCHID CONSERVATION

It is of grave importance that orchid enthusiasts know the origin of each plant they acquire. Tropical forests, the native habitat of most cultivated orchids, are currently the most threatened habitat in the world, in spite of their critical importance to life on Earth. Their lush growth produces much of the oxygen in our atmosphere and, in the process, removes a great deal of the excess carbon dioxide, implicated in the potentially disastrous global warming phenomenon, that spews daily from the homes, factories and cars of developed countries. Tropical forests also support the greatest diversity of life in any known terrestrial ecosystem. Biodiversity, as this is called, is the key to a healthy planet, now and in the future. Every day, many species indigenous to tropical forests are lost before they have even been discovered and classified. It is impossible to calculate the severity of such losses.

Citizens of the impoverished nations in which most tropical forests are found are concerned with filling their bellies and surviving for another day. Many live by the "slash and burn" technique, clearing a patch of lush forest for gardens or to raise livestock (much of which, incidentally, ends up in Western supermarkets or fast-food restaurants). The thin soil of such areas, dependent upon a constant rain of organic matter from the forest and its rapid, year-round decomposition to replenish nutrients, is soon exhausted, and the farmer must move on and clear a new patch of forest. The ecological balance of tropical forests is so delicate that, once cleared and farmed, that area may never support another tropical forest, even if restoration is attempted.

Orchid growers and enthusiasts should not contribute to the depletion of tropical forest species. Never buy orchids which you suspect were collected in the wild; buy only those you are fairly certain have been propagated in greenhouses. If the plants are wilted, damaged or otherwise in questionable health, this indicates that they may well have been recently collected in their native habitat. Most dealers know, or can find out, the origins of their plants. If they balk or give evasive answers to your questions, take your business elsewhere.

Jungle collected orchids at a nursery in the Philippines.

Dendrobium hybrids ready for the auctions.

Inform the merchant of your suspicions and your reasons for not buying plants of doubtful origin.

One can also help conserve tropical forests and their orchids by supporting international conservation organizations. Other measures include buying renewable tropical forest products, such as fruit and nuts, and avoiding products made from tropical hardwoods like teak, mahogany and ebony.

– INTERNATIONAL BODIES AND – – THE ORCHID TRADE –

The Convention on International Trade in Endangered Species of Wild Fauna and Flora (CITES) came into being in 1975. The parties to the Convention agreed to monitor the trade in orchid species around the world, by implementing a permit scheme governing the import and export of plants. Over 100 nations joined the scheme and set up departments to deal with the new regulations. Each country, however, interpreted the regulations differently, leading some to create various loopholes and others to put up obstacles.

CITES has proved detrimental to the introduction of new species to leading commercial hybridists in some countries. Some botanists and conservationists claim that these have been almost totally cleared from the forests where they grow. Yet the hybridists who could multiply these plants have frequently been refused import permits.

In 1990, CITES issued new regulations governing trade in *Paphiopedilum* species. It had earlier declared that these were becoming extremely rare and that many of the 80 or so species were endangered, even though some botanists disputed this. Shortly before the new regulations came into force, orchid nurseries claiming to be traders in forest-collected plants bought up to three times their normal annual purchases of *Paphiopedilum* species, to beat the deadline and to be able to continue trading in the plants afterwards. This has been a blow to conservationists, as the collectors, their traditional livelihoods threatened, probably gathered the plants to the point of extinction.

– HOW TO USE THIS BOOK –

This book is laid out so as to provide a concise and clear guide to identifying orchids. The introduction contains general cultural information on the various orchid genera covered, while the identifier section has detailed entries on the most popular and commonly cultivated orchids, accompanied by a picture of the orchid. Arranged alphabetically within their major groups, each entry gives the family, subfamily and tribe name, as well as the orchid's origin, light and temperature range, its blooming period and cultivation requirements. The symbols below, which accompany each entry, provide vital information at a glance on light, blooming period, ideal temperature (night and day), flower size and cultivation.

LIGHT

FULL SUN

PARTIAL SUN i.e. full shade part of the day, full sun part of the day

DAPPLED LIGHT

FULL SHADE

BLOOMING PERIOD

4-petal symbol representing the four seasons. Shaded petals represent approximate blooming period.

SPRING

WINTER SUMMER

AUTUMN

IDEAL TEMPERATURE

Indication of ideal temperature is given for both day and night, in Fahrenheit and Centigrade.

65–85°F
18–29°C

DAY

55–65°F
13–18°C

NIGHT

FLOWER SIZE

Divided into small, medium and large.

SMALL = ½–2in
(1–5cm)

MEDIUM = 2–5in
(5cm–12.5cm)

LARGE = over 5in
(over 12.5cm)

CULTIVATION

Three different methods of cultivation.

POT

BASKET

LOGS, RAFTS OR SLABS

CATTLEYAS
and relatives

Cattleya and its relatives is by far the most popular group of orchids among enthusiasts world-wide. It was discovered by accident when some plants of the later-named species *Cattleya labiata* were used as packing material for a shipment of mosses and lichens sent from Brazil to the UK in 1818. William Cattley, the noted horticulturist who received the shipment, recognized the unusual nature of the withered plants and nursed them back to health. They first bloomed in 1824 and were found to be an entirely new genus. The native habitat of *Cattleya labiata* was unknown and it was not found again until 1891, when the discovery of a huge population, combined with a higher survival rate due to faster transit, brought the price of orchids within the means of average citizens and launched the boom in orchid cultivation. *Cattleya* species are all epiphytic, naturally growing on trees and rocks in the wild. Depending upon the species, the pseudobulbs grow up to 3ft (90cm) long and are either cane-like or club shaped, with 1 to 3 thick, rigid leaves originating at the top. The sepals are similar to, but slenderer than, the petals; the lip generally has two side lobes, often folded around the column, and a spreading middle lobe. The plain column bears four pollinia, two in each of the anther's two sacs. Most *Cattleya* species have a pleasant fragrance.

There are two basic categories of *Cattleya* species: the labiata, or unifoliates, which bear only one leaf per pseudobulb; and the bifoliates, which generally bear two, and occasionally three, leaves per pseudobulb. Unifoliate *Cattleya* species bear 2 to 6 large flowers with showy lips. Bifoliate flowers are usually smaller but more abundant, with slenderer parts, a fiddle-shaped lip contrasting with the rest of the flower and a very thick, waxy texture. They are often brilliantly coloured and boldly marked with a broad spectrum of hues. *Cattleya* species are cross-bred extensively with other genera to produce hardy, attractive hybrids.

Cattleyas thrive in a household environment, with night temperatures of 65–80°F (18–27°C), or 70–85°F (21–29°C) for bifoliates, and day temperatures of 70–80°F (21–27°C), or 75–85°F (24–29°C). They are sun lovers and bloom more profusely with a southern or western exposure where they receive

about 2,000 foot-candles in summer and up to 4,000 in the winter. Grow *Cattleya* species in relatively small pots with an osmunda or fir bark medium. Water copiously until the excess runs out the bottom, then allow the medium to dry briefly between waterings. Plants in bark need watering more frequently than those in osmunda; they should be fertilized twice a month during spring and summer and once a month in autumn. Those in osmunda need only be fertilized once a month in summer. Mist frequently and provide extra ventilation during periods of extreme heat. In winter, keep the compost barely moist. *Cattleya* species like a relative humidity of about 50% in winter and 70% in summer.

Other members of the subtribe include the genera *Laelia*, *Rhycholaelia*, *Schomburgkia*, *Brassavola*, *Epidendrum*, *Encyclia* and others. All thrive under *Cattleya* conditions.

BRASSAVOLA NODOSA SUBFAMILY EPIDENDROIDEAE TRIBE EPIDENDREAE

65–75°F
18–24°C

55–60°F
13–16°C

A single narrow, fleshy, stiff leaf grows from each short, cylindrical pseudobulb of *B. nodosa*. Each leaf is 10–12in (25–30cm) long with a channelled upper surface. A pendulous inflorescence produces long-lasting white to pale green flowers up to 3in (7.5cm) in diameter, each with a white lip flecked with purple at the base. Flowers are fragrant in the evening.
ORIGIN Southern Mexico, Central America, Venezuela, Peru and the West Indies
TEMPERATURES Day 65–75°F (18–24°C), night 55–60°F (13–16°C)
LIGHT Filtered sun
BLOOMING PERIOD Variable, usually winter to spring
CULTIVATION Grow this orchid in a basket or on a raft. Water generously during the growing period, then gradually reduce the amount of water until new growth begins, but don't stop watering.

CATTLEYA AMETHYSTOGLOSSA SUBFAMILY EPIDENDROIDEAE TRIBE EPIDENDREAE

65–72°F
18–22°C

60–65°F
16–18°C

Flowers of this species are grouped 5 to 8 in a cluster. Each bloom is 3.5–5in (9–12.5cm) across, with white sepals and petals tinted rose-purple and violet-spotted. The lip has a broad, rounded middle lobe with radiating ridges and smaller, upright side lobes. These are tall plants with slim pseudobulbs up to 3ft (90cm) long bearing pairs of leathery leaves each 6–12in (15–30cm) long at the tips.
ORIGIN Brazil, discovered in 1862
TEMPERATURES Day 65–72°F (18–22°C), night 60–65°F (16–18°C)
LIGHT Bright filtered sun
BLOOMING PERIOD Summer
CULTIVATION Same as for *Cattleya aurantiaca*.

CATTLEYA AURANTIACA SUBFAMILY **EPIDENDROIDEAE** TRIBE **EPIDENDREAE**

Two or three leathery leaves originate from each slender pseudobulb. Numerous orange, yellowish-orange or reddish-orange flowers, often with brown, red or purple markings on the lips, are produced on a drooping inflorescence. Each aromatic flower is 1.5–2in (3.7–5cm) long and waxy.

ORIGIN Central America and tropical South America

TEMPERATURES Day 70–75°F (22–24°C), night 60–65°F (16–18°C)

LIGHT Bright filtered sun

BLOOMING PERIOD Late autumn to early spring

CULTIVATION Grow in small pots filled with fir bark or osmunda fibre. Mist frequently and keep in a well-ventilated area. In warmer months, flood pot when watering but allow potting medium to dry out briefly between waterings; in winter, keep the plant barely moist. Fertilize plants in fir bark twice a month in spring and summer, and once a month in autumn; fertilize plants grown in osmunda only once a month in summer. Every three years, repot and support recently repotted pseudobulbs with a bamboo stake.

  | 70–75°F 22–24°C | 60–65°F 16–18°C |

CATTLEYA BOWRINGIANA SUBFAMILY **EPIDENDROIDEAE** TRIBE **EPIDENDREAE**

A cane-like stem, swollen at its base, produces up to 20 flowers. Each flower is less than 3in (7.5cm) across with rose-purple petals and sepals, and a deep violet lip with a white throat.

ORIGIN Belize, discovered in 1884

TEMPERATURES Day 65–72°F (18–22°C), night 60–65°F (16–18°C)

LIGHT Bright filtered sun

BLOOMING PERIOD Autumn

CULTIVATION Basically the same as for *C. aurantiaca* but needs more water. It has a short dormant period in mid-winter.

65–72°F 18–22°C
60–65°F 16–18°C

CATTLEYA DOWIANA SUBFAMILY **EPIDENDROIDEAE** TRIBE **EPIDENDREAE**

Two to six fragrant, yellow flowers occur on a stem, each 6–7in (15–17.5cm) across with a gold-veined purple lip. A single, leathery leaf grows from the apex of each medium-length pseudobulb.

ORIGIN Costa Rica, discovered in 1848
TEMPERATURES Day 65–72°F (18–22°C), night 55–60°F (13–16°C)
LIGHT Bright filtered sun
BLOOMING PERIOD Late summer and autumn
CULTIVATION Same as for *C. aurantiaca*. Provide a winter rest period.

   65–72°F 18–22°C 55–60°F 13–16°C

CATTLEYA GUTTATA SUBFAMILY **EPIDENDROIDEAE** TRIBE **EPIDENDREAE**

70–75°F 22–24°C

60–65°F 16–18°C

Each slender pseudobulb bears two leathery leaves 5–9in (12.5–22.5cm) long. The inflorescence produces 5 to 10 aromatic waxy green flowers, each with brownish-red to deep purple markings and a white and pink lip.

ORIGIN Central America and tropical South America
TEMPERATURES Day 70–75°F (22–24°C), night 60–65°F (16–18°C)
LIGHT Bright filtered sun
BLOOMING PERIOD Autumn
CULTIVATION Same as for *Cattleya aurantiaca*

– CATTLEYA LABIATA –

The "labiata", the showy feature for which this species is named, means "lip". Many of the earliest discoveries in the *Cattleya* genus, which were originally thought to be separate species, are now considered by most botanists to be varieties of *Cattleya labiata*. (These include *C. dowiana, C. eldorado, C. gaskelliana, C. lawrenceana, C. lueddemanniana, C. mendelii, C. mossiae, C. percivaliana, C. rex, C. schroederae, C. trianaei, C. warneri,* and *C. warscewiczii.*) The varieties of *C. labiata*, along with the species *C. luteola* and *C. maxima*, are collectively referred to as the "labiata group", also known as the "unifoliate group" because they bear only a single leaf per pseudobulb. All other species of Cattleyas fall into the "bifoliate group", whose members produce usually two (but sometimes three) leaves per pseudobulb. While *Cattleya labiata* is still reported to be widely grown, the other unifoliate species are becoming scarcer on the commercial market, reflecting the demand for their more luxurious hybrids and for the greater variety of the bifoliate group.

CATTLEYA LABIATA SUBFAMILY EPIDENDROIDEAE   TRIBE EPIDENDREAE

Each pseudobulb produces a single erect, leathery leaf from its apex. The inflorescence bears 2 to 6 large (7in, 17.5cm) rose or pink flowers simultaneously. Each has a magenta lip with an ornately ruffled margin and a yellow throat streaked with purple. They have a pleasant smell.

ORIGIN Central American and tropical South America
TEMPERATURES Day 65–72°F (18–22°C), night 55–60°F (13–16°C)
LIGHT Bright filtered sun
BLOOMING PERIOD Late autumn to early spring
CULTIVATION Same as for *Cattleya aurantiaca*.

   65–72°F 18–22°C 55–60°F 13–16°C

CATTLEYA INTERMEDIA SUBFAMILY **EPIDENDROIDEAE** TRIBE **EPIDENDREAE**

65–72°F
18–22°C

60–65 F
16–18 C

This orchid's flowers, which are 4–5in (10–12.5cm) across, range from milky white to pink in colour and may be violet-speckled. The smooth side lobes of the lip envelop the column in a long tube; the broad middle lobe is coloured a rich amethyst and has an undulating margin. The blooms occur in a cluster of 4 or 5.

ORIGIN Brazil, discovered in 1824
TEMPERATURES Day 65–72°F (18–22°C), night 60–65°F (16–18°C)
LIGHT Bright filtered sun
BLOOMING PERIOD Summer
CULTIVATION Same as for *C. aurantiaca.*

CATTLEYA LODDIGESII SUBFAMILY **EPIDENDROIDEAE** TRIBE **EPIDENDREAE**

70–75°F
21–24°C

60–65 F
16–18 C

A beautiful medium rose colour, this orchid has petals broader than its sepals. The middle lobe of its lip has an undulating margin and several thick, heavy ridges, while the side lobes are plain and turn outward. Two or three thick, hard leaves are borne at the top of the slender pseudobulbs.
ORIGIN Brazil
TEMPERATURES Day 70–75°F (21–24°C), night 60–65°F (16–18°C)
LIGHT Bright filtered sun
BLOOMING PERIOD Summer and early autumn
CULTIVATION Same as for *Cattleya aurantiaca.*

CATTLEYA PERCIVALIANA SUBFAMILY **EPIDENDROIDEAE** TRIBE **EPIDENDREAE**

Measuring 4–5in (10–12.5cm) across, these fragrant flowers vary in colour from light to deep rose. The lip is rather short, with a pale, elegantly ruffled border darkening to a rich burgundy centre. It has an orange throat mottled with deep violet. Each medium-length pseudobulb bears a single, erect, leathery leaf at the apex.

ORIGIN Venezuela, discovered in 1882
TEMPERATURES Day 65–72°F (18–22°C), night 55–60°F (13–16°C)
LIGHT Bright filtered sun
BLOOMING PERIOD Early winter
CULTIVATION Basically the same as for *C. aurantiaca*. May begin new growth immediately after flowering with no rest period.

65–72°F
18–22°C

55–60°F
13–16°C

CATTLEYA SKINNERI SUBFAMILY **EPIDENDROIDEAE** TRIBE **EPIDENDREAE**

This is the national flower of Costa Rica, where it is known as the Flower of San Sebastian. Two or three leathery leaves originate from each of its slender pseudobulbs. Four to twelve waxy rose-purple flowers with white throats and pleasant aromas are produced on the inflorescence. They have a sparkling, crystalline appearance and are approximately 3.5in (9cm) wide.

ORIGIN Mexico and Central America
TEMPERATURES Day 70–75°F (21–24°C), night 60–65°F (16–18°C)
LIGHT Bright filtered sun
BLOOMING PERIOD Late autumn to early spring
CULTIVATION Same as for *Cattleya aurantiaca*.

  70–75°F 21–24°C 60–65°F 16–18°C

ENCYCLIA COCHLEATA SUBFAMILY **EPIDENDROIDEAE** TRIBE **EPIDENDREAE**

E. cochleata varies in size. Its pseudobulbs are egg shaped, somewhat flattened side to side, and 2–8in (5–20cm) long. From the tip of each grow 2 to 3 elliptical or lance-shaped leaves which are 8–12in (20–30cm) long and flexible. Inflorescences also grow from the pseudobulb tips and eventually exceed 20in (50cm) in length, with upside-down flowers which open in succession. Pale green sepals and petals dangle like octopus arms from a concave, shell-like lip striped with green and dark purple.

ORIGIN Florida, West Indies, Central America, Colombia and Venezuela

TEMPERATURES Day 65–72°F (18–22°C), night 55–60°F (13–16°C)

LIGHT Bright filtered sun

BLOOMING PERIOD All year

CULTIVATION Treat this orchid like a *Cattleya*. Grow in a pot with bark or osmunda chopped into medium-sized pieces. Water regularly throughout the year.

ENCYCLIA MARIAE SUBFAMILY **EPIDENDROIDEAE** TRIBE **EPIDENDREAE**

This is a small to medium-sized plant with egg-shaped pseudobulbs only 1.5–2in (3.7–5cm) long. From each pseudobulb tip grow 2 to 3 elliptical leaves measuring 4–8in (10–20cm) as well as an arching inflorescence 6–8in (15–20cm) long with 1 to 4 pale green flowers. The fragrant flowers are long lived and each has a huge showy white lip with green veins in the throat.

ORIGIN Mexico

TEMPERATURES Day 65–72°F (18–22°C), night 55–60°F (13–16°C)

LIGHT Bright filtered sun

BLOOMING PERIOD Summer

CULTIVATION *E. mariae* grows under *Cattleya* conditions or slightly cooler. Raise this orchid in a pot or hanging basket with compost, or on a cork slab. Water regularly during the growth stage, then taper off to a dry winter rest period.

EPIDENDRUM IBAGUENSE SUBFAMILY **EPIDENDROIDEAE** TRIBE **EPIDENDREAE**

This large vine-like plant lacks pseudobulbs but its erect, branching, cane-like stems with aerial roots grow to a height of 3ft (90cm) or more. It has widely spaced alternate leaves which are elliptical, about 4in (10cm) long and leathery. Dense, globular inflorescences grow on the tips of slender stems rising well above the foliage. The flowers, which open in succession, are 1–1.5in (2.5–3.7cm) across, vary in colour from red to orange to yellow, and have waxy sepals and ornately fringed lips.

ORIGIN Central America and South America
TEMPERATURES Day 65–72°F (18–22°C), night 55–60°F (13–16°C)
LIGHT Bright filtered sun
BLOOMING PERIOD Variable throughout the year
CULTIVATION Grows well under *Cattleya* conditions. Pot in any compost, but preferably bark, and water regularly. Support the weak stems with bamboo stakes. When blooms fade, cut the stems back to within one or two joints of the substrate. Propagated by detaching lateral shoots and repotting them.

    65–72°F 18–22°C · 55–60°F 13–16°C ·

LAELIA ANCEPS SUBFAMILY **EPIDENDROIDEAE** TRIBE **EPIDENDREAE**

The oval, elongated pseudobulbs are 4–5in (10–12.5cm) tall and slightly compressed to form sharp ridges. Each bears a single leaf. Jointed, arching inflorescences, up to 3ft (90cm) long, produce 2 to 5 star-shaped, rose-lavender flowers with a brilliant three-lobed lip which is purple outside and yellow with red markings inside. The flowers are 4in (10cm) across and long lasting.

ORIGIN Mexico
TEMPERATURES Day 65–72°F (18–22°C), night 55–60°F (13–16°C)
LIGHT Bright filtered sun
BLOOMING PERIOD Spring
CULTIVATION *L. anceps* thrives under *Cattleya* conditions. Grow it in a pot or hanging basket with bark compost or osmunda fibre. Water regularly but allow the potting medium to dry thoroughly between waterings, especially when not flowering or actively producing new growth.

   65–72°F 18–22°C · 55–60°F 13–16°C ·

LAELIA FLAVA SUBFAMILY **EPIDENDROIDEAE** TRIBE **EPIDENDREAE**

The slender, cylindrical pseudobulbs of this medium-sized orchid are 4–8in (10–20cm) tall and grouped together on the rhizome. Each bears an erect, lance-shaped leaf which is stiff and fleshy. Four to ten yellow or orange-yellow 1in (2.5cm) flowers are borne on the end of an inflorescence 12–16in (30–40cm) long. The lip of each aromatic flower has blunt side lobes and a ruffled middle lobe with four elevated ridges.

ORIGIN Brazil

TEMPERATURES Day 65–72°F (18–22°C), night 55–60°F (13–16°C)

LIGHT Bright filtered sun

BLOOMING PERIOD Spring

CULTIVATION *Cattleya* conditions suit *L. flava* best. Grow it in a pot with bark or tree-fern fibre. Water regularly during the growth period, allowing the substrate to dry out between waterings. After flowering, stop watering for several weeks, then water infrequently. When new growth begins again, resume regular watering. Repot only when necessary.

65–72°F 18–22°C   55–60°F 13–16°C

LAELIA GOULDIANA SUBFAMILY **EPIDENDROIDEAE** TRIBE **EPIDENDREAE**

65–72°F 18–22°C

55–60°F 13–16°C

At the apex of its elongated, pear-shaped pseudobulbs which stand about 6in (15cm) tall, this medium-sized plant produces 2 to 3 stiff, lance-shaped leaves roughly 6in (15cm) long with a leathery texture. This is also the origin of an inflorescence with a terminal cluster of 3in (7.5cm), long-lasting purple flowers. The lip of each aromatic flower has a white throat with purple and yellow markings.

ORIGIN Mexico

TEMPERATURES Day 65–72°F (18–22°C), night 55–60°F (13–16°C)

LIGHT Bright filtered sun

BLOOMING PERIOD Winter

CULTIVATION Raise *L. gouldiana* in a hanging basket with bark or osmunda fibre or on blocks of tree fern. Water regularly during the growth period, allowing the substrate to dry out between waterings. After flowering, gradually reduce the amount of water so that the substrate dries out slowly. Resume regular watering when new growth begins. This orchid appreciates the same environment as *Cattleyas*.

RHYCHOLAELIA DIGBYANA SUBFAMILY **EPIDENDROIDEAE** TRIBE **EPIDENDREAE**

Slender pseudobulbs, compressed and about 6in (15c) tall, each produce a single stiff, fleshy, elliptical leaf which may reach 8in (20cm) in length. Rising from each leaf axil is a stem bearing a single, large, greenish-white flower with a waxy texture and a satiny sheen. The whitish lip is up to 4in (10cm) wide and intricately fringed about the margin. The sepals and petals are relatively slender, their greenish coloration tinted with lavender.

ORIGIN Honduras, Guatemala and Mexico
TEMPERATURES Day 65–75°F (18–24°C), night 55–60°F (13–16°C)
LIGHT Partial sun
BLOOMING PERIOD Spring or summer
CULTIVATION *R. digbyana* grows equally well on a tree-fern raft, bark slab or in a medium-sized pot filled with chopped bark of medium consistency. Water copiously during the growth period, then taper off. It likes more light than *Cattleyas*, about 50–60% of full sun.

65–75°F
18–24°C

55–60°F
13–16°C

SCHOMBURGKIA SUPERBIENS SUBFAMILY **EPIDENDROIDEAE** TRIBE **EPIDENDREAE**

The pseudobulbs of this large plant are about 12in (30cm) long, spindle shaped and longitudinally grooved with a pair of lance-shaped, leathery leaves, also about 12in (30cm) long, at the tip of each. Also originating here is a rigid, erect flower stem, often more than 3ft (90cm) tall, with 10 to 20 5in (12.5cm) flowers near the terminus. The lilac-purple petals and sepals are slender, with rounded tips and undulating margins. The three-lobed lip is yellow in the centre with deep purple veins on the side lobes and 5 or 6 toothed crests on the middle lobe.

ORIGIN Mexico, Guatemala and Honduras
TEMPERATURES Day 65–75°F (18–24°C), night 55–60°F (13–16°C)
LIGHT Partial sun
BLOOMING PERIOD Winter
CULTIVATION Thrives under *Cattleya* conditions. Use a large pot with well-drained compost, or raise it on cork or a tree-fern raft. Water frequently during the growing period. A very bright location stimulates flowering. Afterwards reduce watering so the medium dries out in between. Repot only when necessary.

65–75°F
18–24°C

55–60°F
13–16°C

CYMBIDIUMS and relatives

Cymbidium is by far the major genus of this subtribe and the only one, besides *Oeclades* and *Eulophia*, discussed here. Among the most beautiful of orchids, *Cymbidium* species are also very long lasting, keeping perfectly for six weeks to three months, making them quite popular as corsages. *Cymbidium* species are evergreen plants with large, fleshy roots and pseudobulbs which vary greatly in size and shape from one species to another. The pseudobulbs are sheathed with the bases of leathery, grass-like leaves, which remain green for several years and leave their dried bases when they finally fall. Flower spikes with 1 to 30 blooms may be produced from either immature or mature pseudobulbs, and at first resemble vegetative growth. The oval, pointed sepals and petals are of similar size, shape and colour, with the dorsal sepal often bending slightly forward over the lip. The lip itself is fleshy, with side lobes which stand erect, flanking the column, and a downward-curved, boat-shaped middle lobe with one or more ridges. *Cymbidium* generally likes bright sun and summer nights near 55°F (13°C) and rarely over 60°F (16°C). Daytime temperatures should be kept below 85°F (29°C) if possible. Blooming is thought to be triggered by a combination of long, bright days and cool nights. These orchids like more light than *Cattleya*, from 4,000 to 8,00 foot-candles. If this blend of light and temperatures cannot be achieved in a greenhouse, grow them outdoors. Some shade at midday may be needed to avoid burning the leaves. Repot the plants after flowering but only when necessary and provide a short, dry rest period immediately afterwards. Otherwise, do not let the potting medium dry out or become saturated. These orchids need a moderately free-draining medium which retains some moisture. One recommended *Cymbidium* compost is a mixture of equal parts loam, sand and bark. A slow-release fertilizer added to the medium before use may prove beneficial. *Cymbidium* needs good ventilation and a relative humidity of around 50%.

CYMBIDIUM DEVONIANUM SUBFAMILY **VANDOIDEAE** TRIBE **CYMBIDIEAE**

C. devonianum is a small orchid which produces a pendulous inflorescence with 20 or more olive, tawny or dark brown flowers. The rose-pink lip has a dark purple spot on each side. Numerous broadly lance-shaped, fleshy leaves measuring 4–8in (10–20cm) long occur on each egg-shaped pseudobulb. Pleasantly fragrant.

ORIGIN Northern India
TEMPERATURES Day 65–85°F (18–29°C), night 50–55°F (10–13°C)
LIGHT Full sun
BLOOMING PERIOD Spring
CULTIVATION Grow this species in a hanging basket in well-drained, bark-based compost. Train the pendulous inflorescences over the side to prevent them from burrowing into the potting medium. Water regularly in spring and summer, keeping the potting medium moist, then taper off through winter, almost, but not quite, allowing the medium to dry out between waterings. Requires excellent ventilation.

65–85°F
18–29°C
50–55°F
10–13°C

CYMBIDIUM EBURNEUM SUBFAMILY **VANDOIDEAE** TRIBE **CYMBIDIEAE**

The linear leaves of *C. eburneum* are 12–24in (30–60cm) long, narrow and leathery, and they help support the tuft of slender, elongate pseudobulbs. One, two or occasionally three fragrant white or pink-tinged flowers occur on each stem. Each flower measures 3–4in (7.5–10cm) across and has a creamy lip flecked with rose-purple, with a yellow central ridge.

ORIGIN Northern India
TEMPERATURES Day 65–85°F (18–29°C), night 50–55°F (10–13°C)
LIGHT Full sun
BLOOMING PERIOD Late winter to early spring
CULTIVATION Grow this species in a pot with well-drained, bark-based compost. Water regularly in spring and summer, keeping the potting medium moist, then taper off through winter, almost, but not quite, allowing the medium to dry out between waterings. Requires excellent ventilation.

65–85°F
18–29°C
50–55°F
10–13°C

– CYMBIDIUM INSIGNE –

Cymbidium insigne is prized for its vitality, compact growth, and beautiful upright inflorescences, which may reach 4 feet (1.2 metres) in height. This species has been crossed with *Cymbidium* Eburneolowianum to produce *Cymbidium* Alexanderi "Westonbirt", and with *C. lowianum* to obtain *Cymbidium* Pauwelsii "Compte d'Hemptinne", two very popular hybrids used frequently in breeding programmes.

Cymbidiums derive their genus name from the Greek root "cymbid", for boat, a reference to the flowers' boat-shaped lip. "Insigne" is a distinguishing mark, presumably a reference to the unique qualities of the species.

CYMBIDIUM INSIGNE SUBFAMILY **VANDOIDEAE** TRIBE **CYMBIDIEAE**

The growth of this orchid is compact but its upright spikes of 12 to 20 flowers may reach a height of 4ft (1.2m). They are 3–4in (7.5–10cm) across and range in colour from rose-lilac to white, with rose spots at the base of the petals and sepals. The lip is rounded and rose-flecked with a yellow keel.

ORIGIN Vietnam
TEMPERATURES Day 65–75°F (18–24°C), night 50–55°F (10–13°C)
LIGHT Partial sun
BLOOMING PERIOD Early spring
CULTIVATION Grow this species in a pot with well-drained, bark-based compost. Water regularly in spring and summer, keeping the potting medium moist, then taper off through winter, allowing the medium almost, but not quite, to dry out between waterings. Requires excellent ventilation.

   65–75°F 18–24°C 50–55°F 10–13°C

CYMBIDIUM LOWIANUM SUBFAMILY **VANDOIDEAE** TRIBE **CYMBIDIEAE**

The leaves of this large plant reach 2–3ft (60–90cm) in length and sheath its 9in (22.5cm) pseudobulbs. Long, arching inflorescences each bear 15 to 35 large, long-lasting flowers. The aromatic, yellowish-green flowers have red or brown veins and a pale yellow lip with a characteristic red V-shaped band.
ORIGIN Northern India, Burma and southern China
TEMPERATURES Day 65–85°F (18–29°C), night 50–55°F (10–13°C)
LIGHT Full sun
BLOOMING PERIOD Late winter to early spring
CULTIVATION Grow *C. lowianum* in a pot with well-drained, bark-based compost. Water regularly in spring and summer, keeping the potting medium moist, then taper off through winter, almost, but not quite, allowing the medium to dry out between waterings. Requires excellent ventilation.

   65–85°F 18–29°C 50–55°F 10–13°C

CYMBIDIUM TRACYANUM SUBFAMILY **VANDOIDEAE** TRIBE **CYMBIDIEAE**

Five to twenty-five fragrant flowers occur on each inflorescence of *C. tracyanum*. The fragrant flowers are yellowish-green with red markings and have yellow lips also marked with red. Narrow, linear leaves sheath the pseudobulbs.
ORIGIN Burma and Thailand
TEMPERATURES Day 65–85°F (18–29°C), night 50–55°F (10–13°C)
LIGHT Full sun
BLOOMING PERIOD Late winter to early spring
CULTIVATION Grow this species in a pot with well-drained bark-based compost. Water regularly in spring and summer, keeping the potting medium moist, then taper off through winter, almost, but not quite, allowing the medium to dry out between waterings. Requires excellent ventilation.

65–85°F 18–29°C

50–55°F 10–13°C

EULOPHIA GUINEENSIS SUBFAMILY VANDOIDEAE TRIBE CYMBIDIEAE

70–85°F
21–29°C
65–70°F
18–21°C

Egg-shaped pseudobulbs, about 2in (5cm) long, are tightly clustered on the rhizome of this terrestrial orchid. Its lance-shaped leaves are 10in (25cm) long with an undulating margin and prominent veins, and the petiole of each leaf sheaths the upper portion of a pseudobulb. Ten or more fragrant pink flowers open in succession to form an inflorescence atop a basal stem roughly 16in (40cm) tall. Each flower has a large, showy pink and white lip with an undulating margin.

ORIGIN Tropical Africa
TEMPERATURES Day 70–85°F (21–29°C), night 65–70°F (18–21°C)
LIGHT Filtered sun
BLOOMING PERIOD Autumn to winter
CULTIVATION Grow *E. guineensis* in a medium pot with a combination of bark and osmunda fibre or sphagnum moss. Water regularly throughout most of the year, tapering off for a one-month dry rest period after the pseudobulbs develop. Repot annually.

OECEOCLADES MACULATA SUBFAMILY VANDOIDEAE TRIBE CYMBIDIEAE

70–85°F
21–29°C
65–70°F
18–21°C

O. maculata is small to medium sized, with egg-shaped pseudobulbs which are about 1in (2.5cm) tall and somewhat compressed. At the apex of each is a leathery, elliptical leaf about 8in (20cm) long with a marbled pattern. One or two erect inflorescences, 12–16in (30–40cm) long, rise from the bases of individual pseudobulbs. These produce numerous small flowers with greenish-brown petals and sepals and a pink and white lip.

ORIGIN Tropical Central and South America and Africa
TEMPERATURES Day 70–85°F (21–29°C), night 65–70°F (18–21°C)
LIGHT Full shade
BLOOMING PERIOD Autumn
CULTIVATION Grow in a small- or medium-sized pot containing equal parts of sphagnum or osmunda fibre and bark. Water regularly throughout the year, decreasing the amount somewhat between growing periods. Repot after blooming.

DENDROBIUMS and relatives

This subtribe includes only six genera, of which the major genus, *Dendrobium*, has more than 1,000 species. It is a tremendously varied group in nearly all aspects but all are epiphytes with tightly clustered new growths originating from a rhizome. The flowers are distinguished by a chin-like mentum formed by the fusion of the lateral sepals with the foot of the column. The dorsal sepal and petals are free. The lip, with a spreading or pointed, and sometimes fringed, middle lobe, has side lobes usually enveloping the short column, and its narrow base is attached to the base of the column foot.

Dendrobium species, as indicated by their diversity, come from a variety of habitats in south-western Asia, the Pacific Islands, Australia and New Zealand; their cultivation requirements vary accordingly. All need good light (as much as or more than *Cattleyas*), good ventilation and abundant water during periods of active growth. Otherwise, each species needs individual attention to thrive and flower. Osmunda is a good medium for their fine, wiry roots. Upright species may be grown in relatively small pots, while those that droop will do better in baskets hung high in the greenhouse. They may also be mounted on tree-fern slabs or logs, or on cork slabs.

DENDROBIUM CHRYSOTOXUM SUBFAMILY EPIDENDROIDEAE TRIBE EPIDENDREAE

65–72°F
18–22°C

55–60°F
13–16°C

Slender, ribbed, spindle-shaped pseudobulbs 6–15in (15–37.5cm) long are clustered tightly at the base of this medium-sized orchid. Three to eight elliptical or lance-shaped leathery leaves, each roughly 4in (10cm) long, originate at the tip of each pseudobulb. The inflorescence is erect or drooping and composed of 15 to 20 well-spaced, long-lasting golden-yellow flowers. Each fragrant flower is about 2in (5cm) wide and has a round, fringed lip with an orange disc surrounding the throat.

ORIGIN Southern China, north-eastern India and Indochina

TEMPERATURES Day 65–72°F (18–22°C), night 55–60°F (13–16°C)

LIGHT Bright filtered sun

BLOOMING PERIOD Spring

CULTIVATION Raise in small pots. Water generously during the growth period. In autumn, move to a cooler spot with a night temperature of about 50°F (10°C) and water just enough to keep moist. Move to warmer spot when new growth begins. Save old pseudobulbs, as these continue to bloom.

DENDROBIUM LINDLEYI SUBFAMILY EPIDENDROIDEAE TRIBE EPIDENDREAE

65–72°F
18–22°C

55–60°F
13–16°C

Silvery-grey, spindle-shaped pseudobulbs, 2–3in (5–7.5cm) long with four joints, grow in a tight cluster. From the tip of each grows a single, erect, leathery leaf, oblong in shape and 3–4in (7.5–10cm) long. One pendulous inflorescence, 4–8in (10–20cm) long and composed of 10 to 30 vivid yellow or orange-yellow flowers, rises near the tip of each pseudobulb. The long stalked, 1in (2.5cm) wide flowers with squarish lips are well spaced on the inflorescence.

ORIGIN Southern China, northern India and Burma

TEMPERATURES Day 65–72°F (18–22°C), night 55–60°F (13–16°C)

LIGHT Bright filtered sun

BLOOMING PERIOD Spring

CULTIVATION Grow on a block of wood or cork. Water generously and frequently during the growth period, providing ample fertilizer and ventilation. To induce blooming, cease watering for one to two months, move the plant to a brighter location and lower the temperature slightly. Water moderately from flowering until new growth begins.

– DENDROBIUM NOBILE –

This species has more than 80 named varieties, and is the best known and most frequently cultivated of the Dendrobiums. Its leaves are deciduous, and the velvety flowers bloom on the leafless canes from the previous year.

With more than 1,500 species and thousands of hybrids, Dendrobiums are quite possibly the largest orchid subtribe. Because of their sheer numbers and extensive native ranges, Dendrobiums vary greatly in their physical characteristics and cultural requirements. All are epiphytic and make new growths each year from a rhizome, and while a few have true pseudobulbs, most have slender, jointed stems resembling canes. The generic name comes from the Greek root for "tree".

DENDROBIUM NOBILE SUBFAMILY **EPIDENDROIDEAE**   TRIBE **EPIDENDREAE**

The erect, knotty pseudobulbs of this medium-sized plant are greenish-yellow and approximately 16in (40cm) long. Each node produces one leathery, oblong leaf, 2–4in (5–10cm) long, which usually lasts for two years. Short, nodding inflorescences, composed to 2 to 4 long-lived, fragrant flowers, sprout from nodes which may or may not have leaves. The 3in (7.5cm) white flowers, their sepals and petals tipped with rose-lavender, each have a round, showy white lip with a purplish-red throat.
ORIGIN Northern India, southern China and Indochina
TEMPERATURES Day 65–72°F (18–22°C), night 55–60°F (13–16°C)
LIGHT Bright filtered sun

BLOOMING PERIOD Winter and spring
CULTIVATION D. nobile should be grown in pots or hanging baskets filled with chopped tree-fern fibre and perlite or very well-drained bark compost. Water and fertilize generously during the growth period. In autumn, when the foliage matures and the immature leaves drop, move the plant to a bright, cool spot (with night temperatures of 45–50°F (7–10°C) for two months and withhold water almost completely, providing just enough to keep the canes from shrivelling. When the flower buds appear well developed, return the plant to its regular location and watering regimen.

   65–72°F 18–22°C 55–60°F 13–16°C

DENDROBIUM PARISHII SUBFAMILY **EPIDENDROIDEAE** TRIBE **EPIDENDREAE**

65-72°F
18-22°C

55-60°F
13-16°C

Slender, drooping pseudobulbs grow 16–24in (40–60cm) long. Somewhat leathery, elliptical leaves up to 3in (7.5cm) long sheath the internodes of the pseudobulbs. Growing from the nodes of the pseudobulbs are pairs of rhubarb-scented, rose-purple flowers, each 2in (5cm) wide, with two maroon spots guarding the throat of the lip.
ORIGIN Southern China and Indochina
TEMPERATURES Day 65–72°F (18–22°C), night 55–60°F (13–16°C)
LIGHT Bright filtered sun
BLOOMING PERIOD Spring and summer
CULTIVATION Grows best in pots or small hanging baskets with very well-drained compost. Water frequently with ample fertilizer during the growth period and keep well-ventilated with much light. When the foliage matures, stop fertilizing and water just enough to keep from shrivelling. Move it to a brighter spot while maintaining night-time temperatures. When flower buds have developed, return the plant to its original location and water moderately. Resume regular regimen when new roots appear.

POLYSTACHA BELLA SUBFAMILY **VANDOIDEAE** TRIBE **POLYSTACHEAE**

65-75°F
18-24°C

55-60°F
13-16°C

Longer than their width, these long-lasting, yellowish-orange flowers open in succession on 4in (10cm) stems rising from the tips of pseudobulbs. Leathery, elliptical leaves, 2–5in (5–12.5cm) long, also originate at the tips of the oval, compressed and tightly packed pseudobulbs.
ORIGIN Kenya
TEMPERATURES Day 65–75°F (18–24°C), night 55–60°F (13–16°C)
LIGHT Filtered sun
BLOOMING PERIOD Winter
CULTIVATION Grow on cork or a bark slab with sphagnum packed around the roots. Water regularly and copiously during the growth period, then reduce frequency so the sphagnum dries out between waterings.

ONCIDIUMS and relatives

Of the 60 or so genera in the subtribe Oncidiinae, this book includes
representatives of ten of the more popular: *Miltonia, Miltoniopsis,
Odontoglossum, Oncidium, Psychopsis, Rossioglossum, Lemboglossum,
Brassia, Trichopilia* and *Cuitlauzina*. Their native ranges are spread from
Bolivia to Mexico, and their natural habitats range from the hot coastal
regions of this area to the cool, misty slopes of the Andes.

Only a few species remain in the genus *Miltonia*, taxonomists having moved
the rest in recent years to other genera. Those left are natives of Brazil and
warmer parts of neighbouring countries. With wandering rhizomes and
well-spaced pseudobulbs, they are suited to cultivation on a mount.
Miltonias thrive in a very warm, humid environment and enjoy the same
light levels as *Cattleya*.

Miltoniopsis was originally part of the genus *Miltonia* and includes species
native to Colombia and Panama. They need excellent ventilation, moderate
humidity and intermediate night temperatures up to 60°F (16°C); they do not
tolerate hot days. Pot them in fine bark or medium tree fern mixed with
perlite. Repot only when necessary, and then only at the start of new
growth. The medium should be kept moist, never dry and never saturated.

Odontoglossum was originally a large genus which has been broken up, with
many of its members redistributed to eight other genera. Apparently, true
Odontoglossums, those with a channelled column and a clawless lip, are
found only in South America. The elevation at which these species occur
naturally indicates their temperature requirements in cultivation: those
from the highest elevations may need refrigeration, while species from
intermediate and lower elevations can pretty much be grown anywhere,
possibly requiring a greenhouse environment. They need as much light as
Cattleya or slightly less, excellent ventilation and copious watering. In
general, pot them in tree fern or bark mixed with perlite.

Central American genera formerly in *Odontoglossum* have a clawed lip, a
boat- or shield-shaped callus and a column lacking a channel. They include,
among others, *Lemboglossum, Rossioglossum, Oncidium* and *Cuitlauzina*.
Most will grow readily within the range of *Cattleya* conditions. Fir bark is
reportedly a good medium for this group.

BRASSIA VERRUCOSA SUBFAMILY **VANDOIDEAE** TRIBE **CYMBIDIEAE**

65–75°F
18–24°C

55–60°F
13–16°C

Two flexible, leathery leaves, 8–16in (20–40cm) long and elliptical in shape, arise from the tip of each egg-shaped pseudobulb. One or two basal inflorescences each exceed 20in (50cm) in length and produce many aromatic flowers which bloom in rapid succession. They have very long, slender, pale green petals and sepals, and a broader white lip, all spotted with darker green and/or red at their bases.
ORIGIN Mexico, Guatemala, Honduras and Venezuela
TEMPERATURES Day 65–75°F (18–24°C), night 55–60°F (13–16°C)
LIGHT Filtered sun
BLOOMING PERIOD Spring
CULTIVATION Grow *B. verrucosa* in a light medium in a pot or basket. Water regularly throughout the year. Divide and repot as necessary.

CUITLAUZINA PENDULA SUBFAMILY **VANDOIDEAE** TRIBE **CYMBIDIEAE**

60–70°F
16–21°C

55–60°F
13–16°C

Formerly *Odontoglossum Pendulum*

Pendulous inflorescences originate from the new growth and produce 10 to 20 flat flowers with sepals and petals which are ear shaped and various shades of white, tan, pink and green. The lip, usually white, is an exaggerated kidney shape with a long, narrow middle.
ORIGIN Mexico
TEMPERATURES Day 60–70°F (16–21°C), night 55–60°F (13–16°C)
LIGHT Bright filtered sun
BLOOMING PERIOD Spring
CULTIVATION *C. pendula* should be raised in small pots of well-drained bark or tree fern and perlite. Keep the potting medium moist through the growing period but fairly dry through winter until new growth starts.

LEMBOGLOSSUM ROSSII SUBFAMILY **VANDOIDEAE** TRIBE **CYMBIDIEAE**

Short stems bear 2 to 5 3in (7.5cm) flowers. Their pointed, creamy to greenish-yellow sepals are flecked with dark brown, and the curled petals are white with several brown spots at their base. The large, round lip is pure white with an undulating margin.

ORIGIN Mexico, Guatemala and Honduras

TEMPERATURES Day 55–60°F (13–16°C), night 45–55°F (7–13°C)

LIGHT Bright filtered sun

BLOOMING PERIOD Winter

CULTIVATION *L. rossii* prefers small pots of well-drained bark or tree fern and perlite. Keep the potting medium moist but not saturated throughout the year. Generally, this genus requires a cool, bright, humid (about 70%) environment with excellent ventilation. Allow the medium to dry out between waterings in winter. Report mature plants after flowering.

55–60°F
13–16°C

45–55°F
7–13°C

MILTONIA FLAVESCENS SUBFAMILY **VANDOIDEAE** TRIBE **CYMBIDIEAE**

Sprouting from the rhizome, the egg-shaped pseudobulbs are 2–4in (5–10cm) long and compressed. There are 2 yellowish-green, apical leaves which are sword shaped, flexible and 8–20in (20–50cm) long. Basal floral spikes produce flowers 2–3in (5–7.5cm) across, with pale yellow sepals and petals and a white, purple-streaked, fiddle-shaped lip.

ORIGIN Brazil and Paraguay

TEMPERATURES Day 65–80°F (18–27°C), night 55–60°F (13–16°C)

LIGHT Bright filtered sun

BLOOMING PERIOD Summer

CULTIVATION Grow in medium-sized pots or baskets of bark and sphagnum, perlite or osmunda fibre. It thrives under *Cattleya* conditions. Water generously and frequently during the growth period, then cut back a bit, especially during long overcast periods in winter. Never let it dry out completely or become soggy around the roots. Repot every one or two years, after new growth starts and during cool weather.

65–80°F
18–27°C

55–60°F
13–16°C

MILTONIA SPECTABILIS SUBFAMILY VANDOIDEAE TRIBE CYMBIDIEAE

The pseudobulbs of *M. spectabilis* are spaced at 1in (2.5cm) intervals and its leaves are yellowish-green. Up to 50 flowers, each borne on a separate stem, open simultaneously on this large plant. The fragrant flowers are large and creamy white, and each has a broad, wavy, rose-purple lip with darker veins.

ORIGIN Brazil

TEMPERATURES Day 65–80°F (18–27°C), night 55–60°F (13–16°C)

LIGHT Filtered sun

BLOOMING PERIOD Summer or autumn

CULTIVATION Grow in medium-sized pots or baskets containing bark and sphagnum, perlite or osmunda fibre. It thrives under *Cattleya* conditions. Water generously and frequently during the growth period, then cut back a bit, especially during long overcast periods in winter. Never let it dry out completely or become soggy around the roots. Repot every one or two years, preferably after new growth starts and during cool weather.

ONCIDIUM CLOWESII SUBFAMILY VANDOIDEAE TRIBE CYMBIDIEAE Formerly *Miltonia Clowesii*

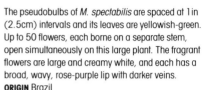

The pseudobulbs, which originate from a branching rhizome, are approximately 3–4in (7.5–10cm) long, egg shaped and compressed. Its two linear leaves are pointed and flexible, and may reach 18in (45cm) in length. Both the sepals and petals are yellow with brown markings, and the distinctively fiddle-shaped lip is purple on the basal half and white on the pointed outer portion. Basal inflorescences may be up to 2ft (60cm) tall with 7 to 10 of these 3in (7.5cm) wide, long-lasting flowers.

ORIGIN Brazil

TEMPERATURES Day 65–80°F (18–27°C), night 55–60°F (13–16°C)

LIGHT Bright filtered sun

BLOOMING PERIOD Autumn

CULTIVATION Grow in medium-sized pots or baskets with bark and sphagnum, perlite or osmunda fibre. Water generously during the growth period, then cut back during overcast periods in winter. Never let it dry out or become soggy around the roots. Repot after new growth starts and during cool weather. Propagate from seed or by dividing the pseudobulbs.

– ODONTOGLOSSUM CRISPUM –

Orchid enthusiasts have often called this species, with its large, crowded sprays of delicately ruffled flowers, the most beautiful of all orchids. Certainly it is the most prestigious and famous of all orchids. *Odontoglossum crispum* is extremely variable, with more than 100 named varieties. Around 1900, finer varieties of this sought-after species brought more than $1,500.00 each, a considerable sum in those days. For its extraordinary beauty, *O. crispum* is the species most often used for hybridization of any in its genus.

The generic name is derived from the Greek roots meaning "toothed tongue", undoubtedly a reference to the toothed projection on the lip. Originating high in the Andes Mountains of South America, these epiphytes demand a cool, humid, well-ventilated environment.

ODONTOGLOSSUM CRISPUM SUBFAMILY **VANDOIDEAE**   TRIBE **CYMBIDIEAE**

Crowded inflorescences of white, pink-tinged flowers, each up to 30in (75cm) long, rise from the bases of oval, compressed pseudobulbs which stand 2.5in (6cm) tall and are densely clustered. The fragrant flowers, which open in succession, may be as much as 3in (7.5cm) in diameter, with broad petals and sepals which have a ragged, ruffled margin. These dwarf the lip, which is also white but with a yellow throat and reddish-brown markings. At the apex of each pseudobulb are 1 to 2 leathery leaves, elliptical or lance shaped and 4–12in (10–30cm) in length.

ORIGIN Colombia
TEMPERATURES Day 55–60°F (13–16°C), night 45–55°F (7–13°C)
LIGHT Bright filtered sun
BLOOMING PERIOD All year but usually winter
CULTIVATION Grow *O. crispum* in small pots of well-drained bark or tree fern and perlite, keeping the potting medium moist but not saturated throughout the year. It requires a cool, bright, humid (about 70%) environment with excellent ventilation. Repot in autumn or early spring.

  55–60°F 13–16°C 45–55°F 7–13°C

ONCIDIUM LURIDUM SUBFAMILY VANDOIDEAE TRIBE CYMBIDIEAE

65–75°F
18–24°C

55–60°F
13–16°C

Both the stiff, mule-eared, 8–20in (20–50cm) leaves and the inflorescences rise directly from the rhizome of this large orchid. The stiff, arching, branched inflorescence may exceed 5ft (1.5m) in length with waxy flowers 1–1.5in (2.5–3.7cm) wide. The petals and sepals are whitish with rose barring and undulating margins. The lip is rose coloured with a white edge, a broadly flared terminal lobe and a yellow crest with pink or orange highlights.

ORIGIN Florida, West Indies, Mexico, Central America, Peru and Guyana

TEMPERATURES Day 65–75°F (18–24°C), night 55–60°F (13–16°C)

LIGHT Filtered sun

BLOOMING PERIOD Spring

CULTIVATION Pot according to size with well-drained bark or osmunda fibre. Water regularly during growing and flowering periods, allowing the medium to dry out almost completely between, and give a short dry rest period once the new growth has developed. *O. luridum* likes some direct sun but needs more shade while blooming.

ONCIDIUM ORNITHORHYNCHUM SUBFAMILY VANDOIDEAE TRIBE CYMBIDIEAE

60–75°F
16–24°C

50–60°F
10–16°C

A small- to medium-sized orchid, *O. ornithorhynchum* produces 1 or 2 arching or pendulous inflorescences from the base of each oval, compressed, 2in (5cm) tall pseudobulb. Crowding the stem, the rose-purple, long-lasting, fragrant flowers are each about 1in (2.5cm) in diameter and have a lobed lip with a yellow crest.

ORIGIN Mexico, Costa Rica, Guatemala and El Salvador

TEMPERATURES Day 60–75°F (16–24°C), night 50–60°F (10–16°C)

LIGHT Filtered sun

BLOOMING PERIOD Autumn and winter

CULTIVATION Use a pot proportional to the plant's size filled with finely chopped fir bark. Water regularly, giving less during cooler periods, and provide a short dry rest period once the new growth has fully developed. This orchid likes some direct sun but needs more shade while blooming. Repot or divide only after the compost has begun to break down.

ONCIDIUM SPHACELATUM SUBFAMILY VANDOIDEAE TRIBE CYMBIDIEAE

Pseudobulbs standing 4in (10cm) tall produce, at the apex of each, 2 to 3 leathery, linear leaves 2ft (60cm) in length. Erect or arching, branched inflorescences originate singly from pseudobulbs and may grow 3ft (90cm) long, each with up to 200 long-lasting flowers opening in rapid succession. Sepals and petals of the 1in (2.5cm) flowers are brown at the base and yellow at the tip, as is the fiddle-shaped lip which has a broadly flared yellow terminal lobe with an undulating margin.

ORIGIN Mexico, El Salvador, Guatemala and Honduras

TEMPERATURES Day 65–75°F (18–24°C), night 55–60°F (13–16°C)

LIGHT Filtered sun

BLOOMING PERIOD Winter and spring

CULTIVATION Can be cultivated in either a pot or basket with any medium; finely chopped fir bark works well. Keep the medium moist but not saturated and provide a short dry rest period once the new growth has fully developed. Likes some direct sun but needs more shade while blooming.

   65–75°F / 18–24°C **55–60°F / 13–16°C**

ROSSIOGLOSSUM GRANDE SUBFAMILY VANDOIDEAE TRIBE CYMBIDIEAE

Formerly *Odontoglossum Grande*

Known as the Tiger orchid. The sepals are narrow and chestnut-brown with yellowish-green barring; the petals are broader, with chestnut-brown bases and yellow tips. The white- or cream-coloured lip is spotted with brown. Four to seven of these flowers, 5–9in (12.5–22.5cm) across, open on each 12in (30cm) inflorescence and last about two weeks. The erect inflorescences rise from the bases of 2in (5cm) tall egg-shaped, compressed pseudobulbs, which also have 1 to 3 leathery, elliptical or lance-shaped, apical leaves up to 16in (40cm) long.

ORIGIN Mexico and Guatemala

TEMPERATURES Day 60–70°F (16–21°C), night 50–55°F (10–13°C)

LIGHT Bright filtered sun

BLOOMING PERIOD Autumn and winter

CULTIVATION Thrives in small pots of well-drained bark or tree fern and perlite. Keep moist but not saturated. It will not tolerate excessive heat or standing water, and requires a cool, bright, humid (about 70%) environment with excellent ventilation.

   60–70°F / 16–21°C **50–55°F / 10–13°C**

– PSYCHOPSIS PAPILIO –

This ornate species is said to be singlehandedly responsible for the world's infatuation with orchids.
Shown at an exhibition of the Royal Horticultural Society, in England, in 1823, it caught the fancy of
the Duke of Devonshire, inspiring him to begin his own orchid collection. Wealthy English noblemen
followed suit, as did the rest of the civilized world.

Formerly belonging to the genus *Oncidium*, this and similar species were reassigned to the genus
Psychopsis in 1836, a move that reflected their unique characteristics. They are commonly known as
Butterfly Orchids, the name being derived from a Greek term meaning "butterfly-like".

PSYCHOPSIS PAPILIO SUBFAMILY **VANDOIDEAE** TRIBE **CYMBIDIEAE**

Formerly *Oncidium Papilio*

Commonly known as the Butterfly Orchid, *P. papilio*
is said to be the species that, upon its introduction to
the UK in 1823, ignited the hobby of orchid
cultivation. Flowers appear on 2–3ft (60–90cm)
stems in succession, with only one at any given time;
they are about 5in (12.5cm) long and 2.5in (6cm)
wide. The petals and dorsal sepal are elongated and
resemble antennae, while the golden lateral sepals
and lip are brown banded. The lip has an undulating,
fine-toothed margin. The green leaves are mottled
with brown.

ORIGIN West Indies
TEMPERATURES Day 65–75°F (18–24°C), night
55–60°F (13–16°C)
LIGHT Filtered sun or artificial light
BLOOMING PERIOD All year
CULTIVATION Use a pot proportional to the plant's size,
filled with finely chopped fir bark. Water regularly,
giving less during cooler periods, and provide a short
dry rest period once the new growth has fully
developed. This orchid likes some direct sun but
needs more shade while blooming.

 65–75°F 18–24°C
 55–60 F 13–16 C

TRICHOPILIA SUAVIS SUBFAMILY **VANDOIDEAE** TRIBE **CYMBIDIEAE**

The flower is most notable for the showy, trumpet-shaped white lip, with deep rose or purple spots and streaks and a scalloped, undulating margin. Its white petals and sepals are fairly slender and mottled with pink. Flowers are borne on a pendulous stem extending horizontally from the base of rounded, flattened pseudobulbs, about 2in (5cm) tall. A single dark green leaf, elliptical, lance shaped, leathery and roughly 8in (20cm) long, grows from the top of each pseudobulb.

ORIGIN Costa Rica, Panama and Colombia
TEMPERATURES Day 65–75°F (18–24°C), night 55–60°F (13–16°C)
LIGHT Full shade
BLOOMING PERIOD Late winter and early spring
CULTIVATION Use a small or medium pot, proportional to the plant's size, and a very well-drained compost. Water regularly during active growth, then stop for three or four weeks and move the plant to a cooler, well-ventilated location. Report annually during this rest period. It tolerates brief periods of direct sun.

65–75°F 18–24°C   55–60 F 13–16 C

Odontoglossum nobile.

PAPHIOPEDILUMS and relatives

Unlike other subfamilies of orchids, Cypripedioideae has not been divided
taxonomically into tribes because it contains only four genera, all
terrestrial. One genus, *Cypripedium*, is native to the temperate zone of the
northern hemisphere and includes the well-known ladyslipper; another
Paphiopedilum, is native to tropical Asia; and two, *Phragmipedium* and
Selenipedium, originated in South America. Only *Phragmipedium* and
Paphiopedilum are commonly cultivated.

Paphiopedilum flowers are extremely long lasting, staying in perfect
condition for a month or even more after being cut. They are inexpensive
and quite easy to cultivate on a window sill and therefore ideal for the
amateur without a greenhouse. The unifying features of this genus are the
pouched lip and the dorsal sepal, which differs significantly from the petals;
otherwise, sepals, petals and foliage are variable.

Cool-growing species, identified by their plain green foliage, like night
temperatures of 50–55°F (10–13°C) and day temperatures of 65–72°F (18–
22°C), never over 85°F (29°C). Warm-growing species, distinguished by
mottled foliage, need night temperatures of 60°F (16°C) or warmer. Both
types thrive under *Cattleya* conditions and can be grown with them as long
as their temperature requirements are met. The best potting medium is fir
bark with pieces 0.5in (1.25cm) large or less, with perlite and charcoal
added. Excellent drainage is essential. Water regularly so that the compost is
never dry nor saturated, and apply enough at each watering so that an excess
drains out the bottom of the pot to flush out harmful accumulated salts. Pot
the plants where they will receive between 1,000 and 1,500 foot-candles of
light in winter and 800 to 900 foot-candles in summer.

Phragmipedium has a dorsal sepal which rather resembles the petals and the
lip has infolded edges, giving it a slipper-like appearance, like *Cypripedium*.
The leaves are smooth and leathery. *Phragmipedium* species need full shade
and copious moisture during the growing season, from spring to autumn.
Repot these orchids in winter and keep them dry until growth resumes.
Osmunda fibre or a mixture of fine bark and perlite make excellent
potting media.

PAPHIOPEDILUM ARGUS SUBFAMILY CYPRIPEDOIDEAE

This orchid's upper sepal is oval, pointed and white with green or green and purple stripes; it may have dark violet spots at the base. The petals are undulating and white with green stripes, purple tips and black warts on the inner surface. A brownish-purple slipper-shaped lip with purple-spotted narrow lobes folded inward completes the blossom. The leathery leaves are mottled.

ORIGIN Philippines
TEMPERATURES Day 65–72°F (18–22°C), night 60–65°F (16–18°C)
LIGHT Full shade
BLOOMING PERIOD Late winter and spring
CULTIVATION *P. argus* thrives under *Cattleya* conditions. Good ventilation is essential. It is best grown in a small, deep pot with a well-drained mixture of fir bark or osmunda fibre, perlite or sphagnum, and charcoal. Water regularly, allowing the roots to become neither saturated nor dry but applying enough for water to run out of the bottom of the pot and flush accumulated salts from the compost. Soon after blooming, divide into clusters of 3 or more and repot.

   65–72°F 18–22°C 60–65°F 16–18°C

PAPHIOPEDILUM BARBATUM SUBFAMILY CYPRIPEDOIDEAE

A single flower, 3–4in (7.5–10cm) wide, grows atop each 10–12in (25–30cm) stem. The upper sepal is white with a green base and maroon or purplish stripes. Fading from green bases to purplish tips, the petals have dark bumps on their upper edges. The slipper-shaped lip is a deep purplish-brown, and the leaves are mottled with dark green.

ORIGIN Malay Peninsula in South-east Asia
TEMPERATURES Day 65–72°F (18–22°C), night 60–65°F (16–18°C)
LIGHT Full shade
BLOOMING PERIOD Summer
CULTIVATION *P. barbatum* thrives under *Cattleya* conditions. Good ventilation is essential. It is best grown in a small, deep pot with a well-drained mixture of fir bark or osmunda fibre, perlite or sphagnum, and charcoal. Water regularly, allowing the roots to become neither saturated nor dry, applying enough for water to run out the bottom of the pot and flush accumulated salts from the compost. Soon after blooming, divide into clusters of 3 or more and repot.

  65–72°F 18–22°C 60–65°F 16–18°C

PAPHIOPEDILUM BELLATULUM SUBFAMILY CYPRIPEDOIDEAE

This species is prized as much for its showy foliage as for its flowers. The dark green leaves, up to 10in (25cm) long and 3.5in (9cm) wide, are dark purple below and mottled with lighter green on the upper surface. Each short stem produces a single round flower up to 3in (7.5cm) in diameter. They are white to pale yellow with dark purple spots.

ORIGIN China

TEMPERATURES Day 65–72°F (18–22°C), night 60–65°F (16–18°C)

LIGHT Full shade

BLOOMING PERIOD Summer

CULTIVATION *P. bellatulum* thrives under *Cattleya* conditions. Good ventilation is essential. It is best grown in a small, deep pot with a well-drained mixture of fir bark or osmunda fibre, perlite or sphagnum, and charcoal. Water regularly, allowing the roots to become neither saturated nor dry, applying enough for water to run out the bottom of the pot and flush accumulated salts from the compost. Soon after blooming, divide into clusters of 3 or more and repot.

   65–72°F 18–22°C 60–65°F 16–18°C

PAPHIOPEDILUM CALLOSUM SUBFAMILY CYPRIPEDOIDEAE

 65–72°F 18–22°C

 60–65°F 16–18°C

This orchid's enormous upper sepal is up to 3in (7.5cm) wide and white with long and short veins which blend from purple at their bases to green above; is folded at the midvein and has a wavy tip. The petals are light green with violet tips and black warts on the upper margins, and the lip is brownish-purple. Each 4in (10cm) flower is borne on a single 15in (37.5cm) stem. The leaves are mottled.

ORIGIN Thailand

TEMPERATURES Day 65–72°F (18–22°C), night 60–65°F (16–18°C)

LIGHT Full shade

BLOOMING PERIOD Spring to summer

CULTIVATION *P. callosum* thrives under *Cattleya* conditions. Good ventilation is essential. Grow in a small, deep pot with a well-drained mixture of fir bark or osmunda fibre, perlite or sphagnum, and charcoal. Water regularly, allowing the roots to become neither saturated nor dry, applying enough for water to run out the bottom of the pot and flush accumulated salts from the compost. Soon after blooming, divide into clusters of three or more and repot.

PAPHIOPEDILUM CONCOLOR SUBFAMILY CYPRIPEDOIDEAE

This orchid produces purple-speckled yellow flowers with a round, concave upper sepal and broad, downward-oriented petals. They measure 2–3in (5–7.5cm) across. The lip is lighter in colour and almost cylindrical, with flattened sides. The leaves are elliptical to oblong, mottled green on the upper surface and scarlet-spotted underneath.

ORIGIN Burma

TEMPERATURES Day 65–72°F (18–22°C), night 60–65°F (16–18°C)

LIGHT Full shade

BLOOMING PERIOD Autumn

CULTIVATION *P. concolor* thrives under *Cattleya* conditions. Good ventilation is essential. Grow in a small, deep pot with a well-drained mixture of fir bark or osmunda fibre, perlite or sphagnum, and charcoal. Water regularly, allowing the roots to become neither saturated nor dry, applying enough for water to run out the bottom of the pot and flush accumulated salts from the compost. Soon after blooming, divide into clusters of 3 or more and repot.

 65–72°F / 18–22°C

 60–65°F / 16–18°C

PAPHIOPEDILUM FAIRRIEANUM SUBFAMILY CYPRIPEDIOIDEAE

This is a small plant with light green leaves. Borne on a 10in (25cm) stem, the medium-sized flowers (2.5in or 6cm across) have a proportionately large upper sepal, greenish-white with a network of violet markings and an undulating margin. Petals droop with recurved tips. They are yellowish-white with markings and margins similar to the upper sepal. The small lip is green and white with purple veins.

ORIGIN India

TEMPERATURES Day 65–72°F (18–22°C), night 50–55°F (10–13°C)

LIGHT Full shade

BLOOMING PERIOD Late summer to autumn

CULTIVATION *P. fairrieanum* thrives under *Cattleya* conditions. Good ventilation is essential. Grow in a small, deep pot with a well-drained mixture of fir bark or osmunda fibre, perlite or sphagnum, and charcoal. Water regularly, allowing the roots to become neither saturated nor dry, applying enough for water to run out the bottom of the pot and flush accumulated salts from the compost. Soon after blooming, divide into clusters of 3 or more and repot.

65–72°F / 18–22°C

 60–65°F / 16–18°C

PAPHIOPEDILUM GLAUCOPHYLLUM SUBFAMILY CYPRIPEDOIDEAE

The leaves of this orchid are bluish-green with a powdery bloom on the surface. The flower has an upper sepal marked with lines of violet dots, spirally twisted petals with amethyst spots and hairy margins, and a slender pink lip with a long narrow base.

ORIGIN Java
TEMPERATURES Day 65–72°F (18–22°C), night 50–55°F (10–13°C)
LIGHT Full shade
BLOOMING PERIOD All year
CULTIVATION *P. glaucophyllum* thrives under *Cattleya* conditions. Good ventilation is essential. Grow in a small, deep pot with a well-drained mixture of fir bark or osmunda fibre, perlite or sphagnum, and charcoal. Water regularly, allowing the roots to become neither saturated nor dry, applying enough for water to run out the bottom of the pot and flush accumulated salts from the compost. Soon after blooming, divide into clusters of 3 or more and repot.

  65–72°F 18–22°C 60–65°F 16–18°C

PAPHIOPEDILUM LAWRENCIANUM SUBFAMILY CYPRIPEDOIDEAE

Bold, deep purple veins reach nearly to the tip of the round, white upper sepal of this large-flowered orchid. Its narrow green petals are violet tipped and have black warts along the margins; the lip is dull purple-green with brown tinges. Mottled yellowish-green leaves adorn the plant.

ORIGIN Borneo
TEMPERATURES Day 65–72°F (18–22°C), night 60–65°F (16–18°C)
LIGHT Full shade
BLOOMING PERIOD Spring to early summer
CULTIVATION *P. lawrencianum* thrives under *Cattleya* conditions. Good ventilation is essential. Grow in a small, deep pot with a well-drained mixture of fir bark or osmunda fibre, perlite or sphagnum, and charcoal. Water regularly, allowing the roots to become neither saturated nor dry, applying enough for water to run out the bottom of the pot and flush accumulated salts from the compost. Soon after blooming, divide into clusters of 3 or more and repot.

  65–72°F 18–22°C 60–65°F 16–18°C

– PAPHIOPEDILUM INSIGNE –

Paphiopedilum insigne is reputed to be the easiest of its genus to grow, making it also one of the most popular. Its most attractive feature is the glossy texture of the flowers, giving them a varnished appearance. One outstanding variety, "Harefield Hall", has been used to produce many hybrids. The flowers of this genus have exceptional keeping qualities, remaining fresh for one month or more even when cut. Paphiopedilums belong to the Cypripedium tribe, whose name is derived from "Cyprus", literally meaning sacred to Venus, and "pedis", the Latin word for foot. The well-known ladyslippers of temperate forests belong to this group, so named for the large slipper-like pouched lip. Members of this tribe are also notable for their dorsal sepals, often broad and boldly marked.

PAPHIOPEDILUM INSIGNE SUBFAMILY CYPRIPEDIOIDEAE

An attractive glossy texture distinguishes the 4–5in (10–12.5cm) flowers of this orchid, which grow singly or, rarely, in pairs, on a 12in (30cm) stem. The upper sepal is broadly oval with an apple-green centre, violet-flecked dark green veins and a white tip. The pale yellowish-green petals have brown veins and an undulating margin, while the slipper-like lip is similarly coloured. It has long, narrow, pale green leaves with a leathery texture.

ORIGIN Nepal and India
TEMPERATURES Day 65–72°F (18–22°C), night 50–55°F (10–13°C)
LIGHT Full shade
BLOOMING PERIOD All year
CULTIVATION Reputedly the easiest member of this genus to grow, *P. insigne* thrives under *Cattleya* conditions. Good ventilation is essential. Grow in a small, deep pot with a well-drained mixture of fir bark or osmunda fibre, perlite or sphagnum, and charcoal. Water regularly, allowing the roots to become neither saturated nor dry, applying enough for water to run out the bottom of the pot and flush accumulated salts from the compost. Soon after blooming, divide into clusters of 3 or more and repot.

  65–72°F 18–22°C 60–65°F 16–18°C

PAPHIOPEDILUM ROTHSCHILDIANUM SUBFAMILY CYPRIPEDIOIDEAE

Huge flowers, more than 8in (20cm) in diameter, in boldly coloured inflorescences of 5 or 6 blooms, are the hallmark of this attractive species. The dorsal and fused lateral sepals are yellow with blackish-purple stripes. Long, slender pale green petals are speckled with purple and veined with dark green. The long, protruding lip is violet with veins of a deeper shade and a yellow top. Leaves are 2–3ft (60–90cm) long.

ORIGIN Sumatra and Borneo

TEMPERATURES Day 65–72°F (18–22°C), night 50–55°F (10–13°C)

LIGHT Full shade

BLOOMING PERIOD Winter

CULTIVATION *P. rothschildianum* thrives under *Cattleya* conditions. Good ventilation is essential. Grow in a small, deep pot with a well-drained mixture of fir bark or osmunda fibre, perlite or sphagnum, and charcoal. Water regularly, allowing the roots to become neither saturated nor dry, applying enough for water to run out the bottom of the pot and flush accumulated salts from the compost. Soon after blooming, divide into clusters of 3 or more and repot.

65–72°F
18–22°C

60–65°F
16–18°C

PHRAGMIPEDIUM CAUDATUM SUBFAMILY CYPRIPEDIOIDEAE

Remarkable for their long petals – up to 3ft (90cm) in length – 3 to 6 of these flowers grow on a flower stem up to 2ft (60cm) tall. The twisted, ribbon-like petals are brownish-yellow with crimson-veined tips, while the twisted lateral sepals are yellow with green veins. A similar dorsal sepal overhangs the white, rose-spotted, pouched lip, which is green at its base and purplish-brown at the tip. The 5 to 7 stiff, erect leaves are up to 30in (75cm) long, bright green, leathery and arranged in a fan shape.

80–85°F
27–29°C

ORIGIN Southern Mexico to Peru

TEMPERATURES Day 80–85°F (27–29°C), night 55–60°F (13–16°C)

55–60°F
13–16°C

LIGHT Filtered sun

BLOOMING PERIOD Spring and summer

CULTIVATION Grow in pots of osmunda fibre, sphagnum or fine bark mixed with perlite. After repotting, keep on the dry side until new growth begins, then water frequently to keep the medium moist. Avoid direct sunlight. Reduce waterings and increase light levels during winter.

PHRAGMIPEDIUM LONGIFOLIUM SUBFAMILY CYPRIPEDIOIDEAE

Six to ten flowers, up to 8in (20cm) wide, grow on a green or purple 2ft (60cm) stem which emerges from the centre of a fan-shaped arrangement of dark green, linear leaves nearly 3ft (90cm) long. Sepals are yellowish-green with darker green veins and white margins, petals are yellowish with purple margins and purple markings near the tip, and the lip margin is V shaped. There are no pseudobulbs.

ORIGIN Southern Mexico to Peru
TEMPERATURES Day 80–85°F (27–29°C), night 55–60°F (13–16°C)
LIGHT Filtered sun
BLOOMING PERIOD All year
CULTIVATION Grow in pots of osmunda fibre, sphagnum or fine bark mixed with perlite. Water frequently and copiously to keep the medium moist. Avoid direct sunlight. Reduce waterings and increase light levels during winter. Repot as needed after flowering, just as new roots begin to grow.

   | 80–85°F 27–29°C | 55–60°F 13–16°C |

PHRAGMIPEDIUM PEARCEI SUBFAMILY CYPRIPEDIOIDEAE

A solitary, long-lasting flower grows atop each erect, downy stem. The pendulous, greenish petals are twisted, with undulating, reddish margins, while the sepals are broader and white with green veins, and the lip is greenish with red spots. The linear leaves are leathery, up to 16in (40cm) long and erect or recurved.

ORIGIN Peru and Ecuador
TEMPERATURES Day 70–75°F (21–24°C), night 50–55°F (10–13°C)
LIGHT Filtered sun
BLOOMING PERIOD All year
CULTIVATION Grow in pots of osmunda fibre, sphagnum or fine bark mixed with perlite. Water frequently to keep the medium moist at all times but do not overwater and do not allow water to stand in the crown. Avoid direct sunlight. Repot mature plants after flowering, just as new roots begin to grow.

 70–75°F 21–24°C
 50–55°F 10–13°C

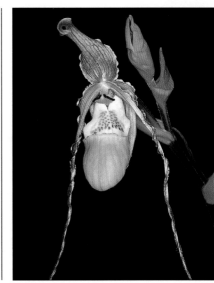

PHRAGMIPEDIUM SCHLIMII SUBFAMILY CYPRIPEDIOIDEAE

A hairy, 12in (30cm) flower stem produces up to 10 fragrant, long-lasting, 3in (7.5cm) blossoms. The oval petals and sepals may be white, greenish-white with a pink tint or deep rose. The egg-shaped lip is white with rose, or possibly violet, spots and veins. The leaves are linear or narrowly lance shaped, about 12in (30cm) long, rigid and leathery, with purple undersides and two unequal lobes at the tip.

ORIGIN Colombia
TEMPERATURES Day 80–85°F (27–29°C), night 55–60°F (13–16°C)
LIGHT Bright filtered sun
BLOOMING PERIOD Spring and autumn
CULTIVATION Grow in pots of osmunda fibre, sphagnum or fine bark mixed with perlite. Water frequently to keep the medium moist at all times but do not overwater. Avoid direct sunlight. Repot mature plants after flowering, just as new roots begin to grow.

  80–85°F 27–29°C 55–60°F 13–16°C

Paphiopedilum niveum *(origin: Thailand)*.

PHALAENOPSIS and relatives

This group includes the genera *Phalaenopsis, Vanda, Renanthera, Sarcochilus, Rhynchostylis, Thrixspermum* and others. As a group, they originate from tropical Asia, the Philippines, Australia and Africa, although individual genera have more limited native ranges.

The plants are epiphytic, usually growing on rocks and trees. Their growth habit is monopodial, meaning that they have no rhizome or pseudobulbs but rather a single, upright stem to which they continually add new leaves at the top and new roots from between the leaves. Inflorescences originate in the leaf axils. Although their large roots, heavy stems and fleshy leaves store some water, they do not tolerate drying as well as orchids with pseudobulbs.

Phalaenopsis, called the moth orchids because of its resemblance to certain tropical moths, is the major genus of this subtribe. The arching foliage, shiny or leathery, plain green or mottled with grey-green and often purple underneath, is arguably as attractive as the flowers. The plants often retain only 5 or 6 of the younger leaves. Tall, arching inflorescences sprout from the axils of the lower leaves on the older portion of the plant, often where the leaves have already been shed. The flowers fall into one of two categories: those with appendages on the lip and petals broader than sepals; and those with similar petals and sepals, lacking appendages on the lip. The lip is united with the column "foot", a basal portion of the column.

In general, the growing season of *Phalaenopsis* is from spring to autumn, and the blooming period is from late summer to winter. Most prefer pots small in proportion to their size and do well in medium or coarse bark, although tree fern, plain or mixed with osmunda, and charcoal chunks also reportedly yield good results. Repot infrequently, as needed but only after flowering when new roots are growing. The ideal night temperature is 65°F (18°C) and it should never drop below 60°F (16°C). Day temperatures should go only up to about 75°F (24°C) in winter but may exceed that in summer as long as precautions, such as misting and shading, are taken against excessive heat. Avoid both desiccation and saturation of the medium, and maintain a humid but well-ventilated environment. *Phalaenopsis* likes about 500 to 1,000 foot-candles of light in summer (5–10% of full sun, less than half that preferred by *Cattleya* species), gradually increased during the autumn to about 1,500 to 2,000 foot-candles in winter.

ANGRAECUM DISTICHUM SUBFAMILY **VANDOIDEAE** TRIBE **VANDEAE**

Only 4–6in (10–15cm) tall, *A. distichum* has a branching tuft-forming stem. The overlapping leaves are triangular, leathery and clasp the stem, completely surrounding it. Many small, fragrant white flowers grow from the leaf axils.

ORIGIN Tropical Africa

TEMPERATURES Day 65–75°F (18–24°C), night 55–60°F (13–16°C)

65–75°F
18–24°C

LIGHT Filtered sun

BLOOMING PERIOD Variable, often more than once a year

55–60°F
13–16°C

CULTIVATION Grow in small pots with fine, light, well-drained compost. Water regularly throughout the year. Provide good illumination. Repot in spring when necessary.

ANGRAECUM SESQUIPEDALE SUBFAMILY **VANDOIDEAE** TRIBE **VANDEAE**

The narrow, linear leaves, 10in (25cm) long or more, are leathery, covered with a light, frost-like bloom and have a bilobed tip. Thick, stiff roots sprout from the aerial portion of the stem. Inflorescences grow from the leaf axils and produce 5 to 6 star-like flowers. Each flower is creamy white, waxy and about 5in (12.5cm) wide with a 10–12in (25–30cm) spur. They are heavily scented, especially at night. Mature plants may grow more than 3ft (90cm) tall.

70–85°F
21–29°C

ORIGIN Madagascar

TEMPERATURES Day 70–85°F (21–29°C), night 65–70°F (18–21°C)

65–70°F
18–21°C

LIGHT Filtered sun

BLOOMING PERIOD Winter

CULTIVATION Raise *A. sesquipedale* in a large pot in well-drained compost. Water regularly throughout the year. Repot only if necessary and be careful to avoid root damage.

JUMELLEA SAGITTATA SUBFAMILY **VANDOIDEAE** TRIBE **VANDEAE**

The 12in (30cm) linear leaves of this large plant overlap and have two unequal lobes and toothed tips. Four-in (10cm) stems originate in the leaf axils, each bearing 1 white, glistening, long-spurred flower with a pleasant aroma.

ORIGIN Madagascar

TEMPERATURES Day 65–85°F (24–29°C), night 65–70°F (18–21°C)

LIGHT Filtered sun

BLOOMING PERIOD Spring

CULTIVATION *J. sagittata* is best raised in a pot or hanging basket in any light, well-drained growing medium. Water regularly throughout the year, tapering off slightly after the growth period.

   65–85°F 24–29°C 65–70°F 18–21°C

PHALAENOPSIS AMBOINENSIS SUBFAMILY **VANDOIDEAE** TRIBE **VANDEAE**

Both petals and sepals are greenish-yellow, orange-yellow or lemon-yellow, with cinnamon-brown barring. Sepals are broader than petals, both are slightly cupped and together they span 2–3in (5–7.5cm). The lip is broadly diamond shaped. The 6–9in (15–22.5cm) inflorescences may be branched and bloom continuously, with 1 or 2 flowers open at a time on each. The 3 to 5 leaves are up to 10in (25cm) long and elliptical to oblong.

ORIGIN Indonesia

TEMPERATURES Day 80–90°F (27–32°C), night 70–75°F (21–24°C)

LIGHT Full shade

BLOOMING PERIOD All year

CULTIVATION Grow in a small pot, using medium-textured chopped fir bark or sphagnum moss mixed with perlite or charcoal. Water regularly to keep the medium very moist but not saturated. Mist on bright days and keep light levels at about half those preferred by *Cattleyas*, increasing during autumn to encourage flowering. It will tolerate morning sun. Repot only after flowering.

 80–90°F 27–32°C
 70–75°F 21–24°C

– PHALAENOPSIS AMABILIS –

One of the most popular species of the genus, and the one upon which the genus is based, *Phalaenopsis amabilis* is the origin of most modern white hybrids prized by collectors for their cascading inflorescences. The first of these was *Phalaenopsis* Elisabethae, a cross between *P. amabilis* and *P. amabilis* var. *rimestadiana*, registered in 1927. Another important hybrid was *Phalaenopsis* Gilles Gratiot, the result of a cross between *P. amabilis* var. *rimestadiana* and *P. aphrodite*. Together, these gave rise to the famous hybrids *Phalaenopsis* Alice Gloria, Cast Iron Monarch, Chieftain, Doris, Henriette Lecoufle, Hermosa, Joseph Hampton, Keith Shaffer, Palm Beach, Polar Bear, Princess Grace, Ramona, Wilma Hughes, Winged Victory, and others. Doris, in particular, had flowers with excellent keeping qualities, and it passed this trait to *Phalaenopsis* Dos Pueblos, Grace Palm, Juanita, and Vallemar, among others. The name of the genus refers to moths, because the open flowers resemble so many moths in flight.

PHALAENOPSIS AMABILIS SUBFAMILY **VANDOIDEAE** TRIBE **VANDEAE**

Tall, arching flower stems bear up to 15 fragrant blooms apiece, each measuring 3–5in (7.5–12.5cm) in diameter. A yellow-tinted lip with crimson spots and streaks accents the pure white sepals and petals. The 3 to 5 pendulous leaves are glossy, dark green and 4–18in (10–45cm) long. This is possibly the most popular member of its genus, and has been used to produce many important hybrids.

ORIGIN Indonesia and north-eastern Australia

TEMPERATURES Day 75–85°F (24–29°C), night 65–70°F (18–21°C)

LIGHT Full shade

BLOOMING PERIOD Autumn and early winter

CULTIVATION Grow in a relatively small pot, using medium-textured chopped fir bark. Water regularly to keep the medium moist but not saturated. Mist on bright days and keep light levels at about half those preferred by *Cattleyas*, increasing gradually during autumn to encourage flowering. It will tolerate morning sun. Repot as necessary but only after flowering and while new roots are developing; water sparingly until the roots are fully developed.

   75–85°F 24–29°C 65–70°F 18–21°C

PHALAENOPSIS APHRODITE SUBFAMILY **VANDOIDEAE** TRIBE **VANDEAE**

The many white flowers of this orchid may be pink-tinted and are borne in a drooping inflorescence. Each has a pink and yellow lip with long, twisted, filamentous appendages projecting from the apex. Brownish-green leaves with purplish undersides are ribbed down the centre and measure 8–16in (20–40cm) long.

ORIGIN Java and Philippines

TEMPERATURES Day 75–85°F (24–29°C), night 65–70°F (18–21°C)

LIGHT Full shade

BLOOMING PERIOD Spring and summer

CULTIVATION Grow this species in a relatively small pot, using medium-textured chopped fir bark or sphagnum moss mixed with perlite or charcoal. Water regularly to keep the medium moist but not saturated. Mist on bright days and keep light levels at about half those preferred by *Cattleyas*, increasing gradually to *Cattleya* levels during autumn. It will tolerate morning sun. Repot as necessary but only after flowering and while new roots are developing; water sparingly until the roots are fully developed.

75–85°F
24–29°C

65–70°F
18–21°C

PHALAENOPSIS CORNU-CERVI SUBFAMILY **VANDOIDEAE** TRIBE **VANDEAE**

Each inflorescence bears up to 12 flowers, with 3 to 5 open at any time. They are 1–2in (2.5–5cm) wide, star shaped, yellowish-green with chestnut bars and waxy in texture. The lip is white. Each plant produces up to 5 yellowish leaves, about 8in (20cm) long, narrow, glossy and leathery.

ORIGIN Thailand, Burma and Java

TEMPERATURES Day 75–85°F (24–29°C), night 62–68°F (17–20°C)

LIGHT Bright full shade

BLOOMING PERIOD All year

CULTIVATION Grow this species in a relatively small pot, using medium-textured chopped fir bark mixed with perlite and sphagnum. Water regularly in moderate amounts to keep the medium moist but not saturated. Mist on bright days and keep light levels at about half those preferred by *Cattleyas*, increasing gradually to *Cattleya* levels during autumn. It will tolerate morning sun. Repot as necessary but only after flowering and while new roots are developing; water sparingly until the roots are fully developed.

75–85°F
24–29°C

62–68°F
17–20°C

PHALAENOPSIS EQUESTRIS SUBFAMILY **VANDOIDEAE** TRIBE **VANDEAE**

These 1in (2.5cm) wide flowers have white-bordered, rose-purple sepals and petals. The lip has white lateral lobes and a midlobe with a brown base, magenta tip and a yellow or white crest. Each of the 3 to 5 fleshy leaves is bright green, oblong, 6–8in (15–20cm) long – and notched at the tip.

ORIGIN Philippines

TEMPERATURES Day 75–85°F (24–29°C), night 62–68°F (17–20°C)

LIGHT Bright full shade

BLOOMING PERIOD All year

CULTIVATION Grow this species in a relatively small pot, using medium-textured chopped fir bark. Water regularly in moderate amounts to keep the medium moist but not saturated. Mist on bright days and keep light levels at about half those preferred by *Cattleyas*, increasing gradually to *Cattleya* levels during autumn. It will tolerate morning sun. Repot as necessary but only after flowering and while new roots are developing; water sparingly until the roots are fully developed.

| | 75–85°F 24–29°C | 62–68°F 17–20°C | | |

PHALAENOPSIS LUEDDEMANNIANA SUBFAMILY **VANDOIDEAE** TRIBE **VANDEAE**

The 2in (5cm) flowers of this orchid are long lasting, fragrant, waxy and star shaped, with sepals broader than petals. They can vary tremendously in colour but are often rose-purple, with or without white markings. The narrow lip is orange and violet with a sharp, raised crest. Leaves are bright yellowish-green, 6–12in (15–30cm) long, narrow and oblong.

ORIGIN Philippines

TEMPERATURES Day 75–85°F (24–29°C), night 62–68°F (17–20°C)

LIGHT Bright full shade

BLOOMING PERIOD All year

CULTIVATION Grow this species in a relatively small pot, using medium-textured chopped fir bark. Water regularly in moderate amounts to keep the medium moist but not saturated. Mist on bright days and keep light levels at about half those preferred by *Cattleyas*, increasing gradually to *Cattleya* levels during autumn. It will tolerate morning sun. Repot as necessary but only after flowering and while new roots are developing; water sparingly until the roots are fully developed.

| | 75–85°F 24–29°C | 62–68°F 17–20°C | | |

PHALAENOPSIS MARIAE SUBFAMILY **VANDOIDEAE** TRIBE **VANDEAE**

Depending upon maturity, a single plant may produce well over 100 blooms simultaneously. Each flower is about 2in (5cm) across and star shaped, with whitish petals and sepals marked with large burgundy or chestnut spots. The lip is purple with a white border. Leaves are glossy green, oblong, 6–12in (15–30cm) long and twisted at the base.

ORIGIN Philippines

TEMPERATURES Day 75–85°F (24–29°C), night 62–68°F (17–20°C)

LIGHT Deep full shade

BLOOMING PERIOD Summer

CULTIVATION Grow this species in a relatively small pot, using medium-textured chopped fir bark or sphagnum moss mixed with perlite or charcoal. Water regularly in moderate amounts to keep the medium moist but not saturated. Mist on bright days and keep light levels at about half those preferred by *Cattleyas*. Repot as necessary but only after flowering and while new roots are developing; water sparingly until the roots are fully developed.

75–85°F
24–29°C

62–68°F
17–20°C

PHALAENOPSIS SANDERIANA SUBFAMILY **VANDOIDEAE** TRIBE **VANDEAE**

Each inflorescence produces only a few 3in (7.5cm) wide flowers. They have rounded petals, a delicate texture and highly variable coloration, from white to magenta. The white lip may have yellow, or cinnamon markings, and a pair of long, filamentous appendages project from its apex. The leaves are about 10in (25cm) long, elliptical to oblong and dark green with a silvery bloom and purplish-brown tint.

ORIGIN Philippines

TEMPERATURES Day 75–85°F (24–29°C), night 62–68°F (17–20°C)

LIGHT Full shade

BLOOMING PERIOD All year

CULTIVATION Pot according to size, using medium-textured chopped fir bark or sphagnum moss mixed with perlite or charcoal. Water regularly in moderate amounts to keep the medium moist but not saturated. Mist on bright days and keep light levels at about half those preferred by *Cattleyas*, increasing during autumn. It will tolerate morning sun. Repot only after flowering and while new roots are developing; water sparingly until the roots are fully developed.

75–85°F
24–29°C

62–68°F
17–20°C

PHALAENOPSIS SCHILLERIANA SUBFAMILY **VANDOIDEAE** TRIBE **VANDEAE**

At up to 100 3in (7.5cm) flowers per inflorescence, this species is quite impressive in bloom. The colour of the petals, sepals and lip is variable, usually white or some shade of pink or rose-purple, and the anchor-shaped lip is red-spotted with magenta side lobes. The leaves are 6–18in (15–45cm) long and a dull dark green, mottled with greyish-white above and purple underneath.

ORIGIN Philippines
TEMPERATURES Day 75–85°F (24–29°C), night 62–68°F (17–20°C)
LIGHT Full shade
BLOOMING PERIOD Spring
CULTIVATION Grow this species in a relatively small pot, using medium-textured chopped fir bark. Water regularly in moderate amounts to keep the medium moist but not saturated. Mist on bright days and keep light levels at about half those preferred by *Cattleyas*. It will tolerate morning sun. Repot only after flowering and while new roots are developing; water sparingly until the roots are fully developed.

   75–85°F 24–29°C 62–68°F 17–20°C

PHALAENOPSIS STUARTIANA SUBFAMILY **VANDOIDEAE** TRIBE **VANDEAE**

There may be hundreds of 3in (7.5cm) flowers on each plant. The sepals are white and the lateral ones are tinted yellow near the base and flecked with crimson, while the petals are white with fine amethyst spots at the base. The lip is sulphur-yellow with a white margin and purple spots. Limp leaves are 12–18in (30–45cm) long and greyish-green above, with magenta undersides.

ORIGIN Philippines
TEMPERATURES Day 75–85°F (24–29°C), night 62–68°F (17–20°C)
LIGHT Full shade
BLOOMING PERIOD Spring
CULTIVATION Grow this species in a proportionately small pot, using medium-textured chopped fir bark or a mixture of sphagnum and perlite or charcoal. Water regularly in moderate amounts to keep the medium moist but not saturated. Mist on bright days and keep light levels at about half those preferred by *Cattleyas*. It will tolerate morning sun. Repot only after flowering and while new roots are developing; water sparingly until the roots are fully developed.

   75–85°F 24–29°C 62–68°F 17–20°C

PHALAENOPSIS VIOLACEA SUBFAMILY **VANDOIDEAE** TRIBE **VANDEAE**

Fragrant, star-shaped flowers with a waxy texture open in succession, usually no more than 2 or 3 at once. There are several different varieties but normally the petals and sepals are pale green with amethyst spots and the lip is purple. Certain varieties are white or rose-purple. The flowers are 2–3in (5–7.5cm) wide, while the leaves are 6–12in (15–30cm) long, glossy, fleshy and egg-shaped.

ORIGIN Borneo and Malay Peninsula
TEMPERATURES Day 75–85°F (24–29°C), night 62–68°F (17–20°C)
LIGHT Full shade
BLOOMING PERIOD Summer and autumn
CULTIVATION Grow this species in a proportionately small pot, using medium-textured chopped fir bark or a mixture of sphagnum and perlite or charcoal. Water regularly in moderate amounts to keep the medium moist but not saturated. Mist on bright days and keep light levels at about half those preferred by *Cattleyas*. It will tolerate morning sun. Repot only after flowering and while new roots are developing; water sparingly until the roots are fully developed.

75–85°F
24–29°C

62–68°F
17–20°C

RENANTHERA IMSCHOOTIANA SUBFAMILY **VANDOIDEAE** TRIBE **VANDEAE**

Erect, 2ft (60cm) stems produce a multitude of alternate leaves which are leathery, oblong, bilobed and up to 4in (10cm) long. From the leaf axils rise branched inflorescences with many showy, long-lasting flowers measuring about 1.5in (3.7cm) across. The petals and dorsal sepal are slender, erect and yellow or creamy white with red spots, while the lateral sepals are much broader, red above and yellow underneath, with undulating margins. The lip is very small.

ORIGIN North-eastern India, Burma and Vietnam
TEMPERATURES Day 65–75°F (18–24°C), night 55–60°F (13–16°C)
LIGHT Full sun
BLOOMING PERIOD Late spring and early summer
CULTIVATION *R. imschootiana* does best in a medium-sized pot with a very well-drained medium such as coarsely chopped bark. Water regularly year round and provide bright midday shade in summer. Do not repot until the medium begins to deteriorate.

65–75°F
18–24°C

55–60°F
13–16°C

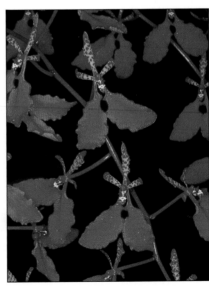

RENANTHERA MONACHICA SUBFAMILY VANDOIDEAE TRIBE VANDEAE

Erect stems no more than 12in (30cm) tall produce alternate, stiff, elliptical leaves about 4in (10cm) long with two unequal lobes at the tips. They are dark green with tinges of purple. The leaf axils give rise to branched inflorescences with long-lasting, 1in (2.5cm) wide flowers which are yellow with red spots and open in quick succession.

ORIGIN Philippines

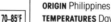

TEMPERATURES Day 70–85°F (21–29°C), night 60–65°F (16–18°C)

LIGHT Bright filtered sun

BLOOMING PERIOD Early spring

CULTIVATION *R. monachica* thrives in a medium-sized pot with a very well-drained medium such as coarsely chopped bark. Water regularly year round. Will also do well in direct sunlight if it is shaded for part of the day. Do not repot until the medium begins to deteriorate.

RHYNCHOSTYLIS GIGANTEA SUBFAMILY VANDOIDEAE TRIBE VANDEAE

Also known as the Foxtail Orchid. A stem, 6in (15cm) or taller, is densely sheathed by the bases of alternate, 1ft (30cm) long leaves with a leathery texture and unequally bilobed tips. Dense, pendulous inflorescences emerging from the leaf axils and extending up to 15in (37.5cm) have earned this and other members of the genus the nickname foxtail orchids. They produce hundreds of white, magenta-spotted flowers with magenta lips, about 1in (2.5cm) wide, long lasting and delightfully fragrant.

ORIGIN Thailand, Burma and Laos

TEMPERATURES Day 70–85°F (21–29°C), night 60–65°F (16–18°C)

LIGHT Partial sun

BLOOMING PERIOD Autumn and early winter

CULTIVATION Grow in a hanging basket with a medium consisting of coarse bark, charcoal and crock. It doesn't tolerate repotting very well, so nest the original basket inside a larger one and fill the space with a similar medium. Place the basket in a well-lit location and water regularly throughout the year.

PLEIONE MACULATA SUBFAMILY **EPIDENDROIDEAE**   TRIBE **COELOGYNEAE**

Single flowers, 2.5in (6cm) in diameter, grow on short stems sprouting from glossy green, 1in (2.5cm), turban-shaped pseudobulbs which have dropped their pair of leaves. The sepals and petals are creamy white, sometimes pink-streaked, and the lip has an undulating margin and a yellow centre with crimson markings. The leaves sprouting from the apex of pseudobulbs are elliptical or lance shaped and up to 10in (25cm) long.

ORIGIN Northern India, Nepal, Burma, southern China and Thailand

TEMPERATURES Day 60–70°F (16–21°C), night 50–55°F (10–13°C)

LIGHT Filtered sun

BLOOMING PERIOD Autumn

CULTIVATION This species prefers a small pot filled with a well-drained medium, such as a mixture of equal parts osmunda fibre, finely chopped bark and sphagnum. Repot after the leaves drop and before the flowers bloom. Keep the medium moist during active growth. Provide a cool, dry rest period in winter. Avoid direct sunlight.

PLEIONE PRAECOX SUBFAMILY **EPIDENDROIDEAE**   TRIBE **COELOGYNEAE**

The 3in (7.5cm) wide flowers with a spicy fragrance usually have a rich rose-purple hue, or they may be white speckled with lilac. The fringed lip is most often a darker shade with a yellow central streak and fringed crests but it may be white or pink with purple spots. A pair of elliptical leaves, 6–10in (15–25cm) long, is produced by each pseudobulb, which is about 1in (2.5cm) long, turban or barrel shaped and green mottled with purple or reddish-brown.

ORIGIN Northern India, Nepal, Burma, southern China and Thailand

TEMPERATURES Day 60–70°F (16–21°C), night 50–55°F (10–13°C)

LIGHT Bright filtered sun

BLOOMING PERIOD Autumn

CULTIVATION Use a small pot filled with a well-drained medium, such as a mixture of equal parts osmunda fibre, finely chopped bark and sphagnum. Repot after the leaves drop and before the flowers bloom. Keep the medium moist during active growth. Provide a cool, dry rest period in winter with night temperatures at or just above freezing. Avoid direct sunlight.

PLEIONE SPECIOSA SUBFAMILY **EPIDENDROIDEAE** TRIBE **COELOGYNEAE**

The 9in (22.5cm) stems, emerging from the bases of pseudobulbs, produce 1 or 2 flowers apiece. Though variable in size and colour, the lightly scented flowers are generally magenta or rose-purple, with white or yellow ridges on the lip. Each 1in (2.5cm) long pseudobulb is roughly textured and produces a single 6in (15cm) leaf.

ORIGIN Southern China

TEMPERATURES Day 65–75°F (18–24°C), night 55–60°F (13–16°C)

LIGHT Filtered sun

BLOOMING PERIOD Spring

CULTIVATION *P. speciosa* likes a small pot filled with a well-drained medium such as a mixture of equal parts osmunda fibre, finely chopped bark and sphagnum. Repot after the leaves drop and before the flowers bloom. Keep the medium moist during active growth. Provide a cool, dry rest period in winter with night temperatures at or just above freezing. Avoid direct sunlight.

   65–75°F 18–24°C 55–60°F 13–16°C

Pleione formosana.

BOTANICALS

Botanicals are a diverse group of lesser-known, but no less fascinating, orchids. They include members of several tribes, and thus are not as closely related to one another as the previously discussed groups. In general, their flowers are smaller and less spectacular than those of the major orchid groups. The group name is derived from the early days of modern orchid cultivation when these genera were rarely grown by hobbyists, and were of interest, therefore, only to professional botanists.

Chief among these are Catasetums and their relatives, often known as "pollen-shooters". Through unknown environmental pressures, these renegades have evolved a unique method of ensuring pollination. A trigger is located within the potently fragrant tissues of each flower so that a visiting insect is certain to disturb it, whereupon a sticky disc of pollen, the pollinarium, is shot towards the insect, splattering on contact and setting instantly to ensure adherence. Pollen-shooters include the genera *Catasetum* and *Cycnoches* (subtribe Catasetinae).

Other botanicals include, but are by no means limited to the genera *Bletilla* and *Phaius* (subtribe Bletiinae), *Gongora* (subtribe Stanhopeinae), *Maxillaria (subtribe Maxillariinae), Pabstia, Pescatorea, Promenaea,* and *Zygopetalum* (subtribe Zygopetalinae), *Sobralia* (subtribe Sobraliinae), and *Thunia* (subtribe Thuniiae).

BLETILLA STRIATA SUBFAMILY **EPIDENDROIDEAE** TRIBE **ARETHUSEAE**

This medium to large terrestrial plant stands 8–24in (20–60cm) tall and has rounded, underground pseudobulbs. Several oblong or lance-shaped leaves grow on an erect stem. The green leaves may have white flecks and are about 2in (5cm) wide, up to 16in (40cm) long, flexible and pleated. Several fragrant amethyst flowers, each about 1.5in (3.7cm) long, grow well spaced on an 8in (20cm) inflorescence and open successively.

ORIGIN China and Japan
TEMPERATURES Wide range
LIGHT Filtered sun
BLOOMING PERIOD Late spring to summer
CULTIVATION *B. striata* is easily grown in a pot or as an ordinary garden plant. Sandy, leafy soil yields the best results but almost any type will do. Apply composted manure in spring. Grow in a sunny location with midday shade. Water generously in spring and summer, then, as the foliage starts to die back, keep barely moist until new growth begins in spring. Hardy in winter to 20°F (−7°C); mulch with straw in colder climates.

CATASETUM BARBATUM SUBFAMILY **VANDOIDEAE** TRIBE **CYMBIDIEAE**

This medium-sized orchid has pseudobulbs about 6in (15cm) tall and membranous, lance-shaped or teardrop-shaped leaves 8–14in (20–35cm) long and 2–3in (5–7.5cm) wide. Inflorescences are basal and of a single sex: the male is rather rigid and arching with many fringed flowers, while the female is short and erect with few hooded flowers. Male flowers have a spring-loaded mechanism which shoots pollen a relatively long distance when tripped. Both sexes are frgrant.

ORIGIN Ecuador, Peru, Bolivia, Brazil and Guyana
TEMPERATURES Day 65–75°F (18–24°C), night 55–60°F (13–16°C)
LIGHT Filtered sun
BLOOMING PERIOD Winter to spring
CULTIVATION *C. barbatum* should be grown in small pots filled with a well-drained potting medium. Water generously during the growing period, then stop once the flowers and deciduous leaves have dropped. Mist occasionally and resume regular watering only when new growth begins.

| 65–75°F |
| 18–24°C |

| 55–60°F |
| 13–16°C |

CYCNOCHES HAAGII SUBFAMILY **VANDOIDEAE** TRIBE **CYMBIDIEAE**

Known as the Swan Orchid, this is a medium-sized orchid with spindle-shaped or cylindrical pseudobulbs measuring 10in (25cm) or longer. Its leaves are 4–12in (10–30cm) long, broadly lance shaped, membranous and pleated. Curved inflorescences arise from leaf axils and simultaneously produce many long-lived green and white flowers, each bearing a remarkable resemblance to a swan.

ORIGIN Brazil

TEMPERATURES Day 70–85°F (21–29°C), night 65–70°F (18–21°C)

LIGHT Filtered sun

BLOOMING PERIOD Autumn to winter

CULTIVATION Raise *C. haagii* in a pot with well-drained compost. Water regularly during the growth period but allow the compost to dry thoroughly between waterings. Repot annually after the deciduous leaves have dropped, then stop watering for several weeks, until new roots begin to develop.

GONGORA TRUNCATA SUBFAMILY **VANDOIDEAE** TRIBE **CYMBIDIEAE**

The pear-shaped pseudobulbs of this medium to large orchid are 4in (10cm) long with deep grooves and are clustered tightly together. Each has two leathery, teardrop-shaped leaves, 10–16in (25–40cm) long, growing from its tip. One or more pendulous inflorescences, often over 20in (50cm) long, originate at the base of each pseudobulb and possess 30 to 40 fragrant, widely spaced flowers. Opening simultaneously, the purple-spotted flowers are long stalked, about 1.5in (3.7cm) across and have a waxy lip which is compressed side to side.

ORIGIN Mexico

TEMPERATURES Day 65–85°F (18–29°C), night 55–65°F (13–18°C)

LIGHT Filtered sun

BLOOMING PERIOD Spring and summer

CULTIVATION Raise *G. truncata* in a hanging basket or pot, with a well-drained substrate of bark, sphagnum or osmunda fibre. It prefers high humidity. Keep it moist during the growth period. When in bud, provide a brief rest period by withholding water and relocating to a cooler, shadier spot.

MAXILLARIA PICTA SUBFAMILY **VANDOIDEAE** TRIBE **MAXILLARIEAE**

A small- to medium-sized plant, *M. picta* has pear-shaped, grooved pseudobulbs, 2–3in (5–7.5cm) tall, clustered on the rhizome. The 1 to 3 linear to lance-shaped leaves on each pseudobulb apex are 10–14in (25–35cm) long, leathery and flexible. Several bracts sheath pendulous or upright flower stems, each bearing a fragrant bell-shaped flower, tawny yellow inside and white spotted with reddish or purplish-brown outside. The flowers are about 2.5in (6cm) wide.

ORIGIN Eastern Brazil
TEMPERATURES Day 65–75°F (18–24°C), night 55–60°F (13–16°C)
LIGHT Filtered sun
BLOOMING PERIOD Autumn and winter
CULTIVATION Raise in a pot or hanging basket; it is not fussy about growing media. Water regularly throughout the year, reducing somewhat once the new growth is fully developed. Provide a three-week dry rest period after flowering. Repot as necessary but preferably at intervals of three to four years.

MAXILLARIA RUFESCENS SUBFAMILY **VANDOIDEAE** TRIBE **MAXILLARIEAE**

The pseudobulbs of this small- to medium-sized orchid are usually elliptical and somewhat flattened. A single elliptical to lance-shaped leaf, erect, leathery and approximately 10in (25cm) long, grows at each pseudobulb tip. Basal flower stems just 2in (5cm) long bear single, somewhat bell-shaped, flowers. The aromatic, red-spotted flowers are usually yellow to burnt orange in colour.

ORIGIN West Indies, Central America and northern South America
TEMPERATURES Day 65–75°F (18–24°C), night 55–60°F (13–16°C)
LIGHT Filtered sun
BLOOMING PERIOD Variable and extended
CULTIVATION Small- to medium-sized pots suit *M. rufescens* best; it is not fussy about growing media. Water regularly throughout the year, reducing somewhat once the new growth is fully developed. Provide a three-week dry rest period after flowering. Repot as necessary but preferably at intervals of three to four years.

PABSTIA JUGOSA SUBFAMILY **VANDOIDEAE**   TRIBE **MAXILLARIEAE**

This orchid's long-lasting flowers are 2–3in (5–7.5cm) in diameter with broad white sepals, rounded white petals striped with red or purplish-red, and a round white lip striped with bluish-amethyst. Its pseudobulbs are 2–3in (5–7.5cm) tall and an elongated egg shape, with lengthwise grooves and two lance-shaped, folded, flexible leaves 6–10in (15–25cm) long.

ORIGIN Southern Brazil

TEMPERATURES Day 70–85°F (21–29°C), night 65–70°F (18–21°C)

LIGHT Partial sun

BLOOMING PERIOD Spring and early summer

CULTIVATION *P. jugosa* is best grown in a medium-sized, well-drained pot filled with bark. Water regularly throughout the year, tapering off slightly after new growth ceases. Divide and repot mature plants as necessary.

   70–85°F 21–29°C 65–70°F 18–21°C

PESCATOREA LEHMANNII SUBFAMILY **VANDOIDEAE**   TRIBE **MAXILLARIEAE**

Short, stiff flower stems rise from leaf axils and bear single, long-lasting, fragrant flowers 2.5in (6cm) in diameter. They have white petals and sepals flushed with purple; the centre lobe of the lip is covered with dense hair. The lance-shaped leaves of this medium-sized orchid are 12–20in (30–50cm) long. Pseudobulbs are lacking.

ORIGIN Ecuador and Colombia

TEMPERATURES Day 65–75°F (18–24°C), night 55–60°F (13–16°C)

LIGHT Bright filtered sun

BLOOMING PERIOD All year, usually in spring

CULTIVATION This orchid likes a medium-sized pot filled with osmunda fibre or medium chopped bark, although tree fern and sphagnum moss have reportedly been used with success. Water regularly to keep the medium moist but not saturated. There is no rest period. Repot only if necessary and if new root growth is evident.

 65–75°F 18–24°C
 55–60°F 13–16°C

PHAIUS TANKERVILLEAE SUBFAMILY **EPIDENDROIDEAE** TRIBE **ARETHUSEAE**

Spikes 3ft (90cm) long bear 10 to 15 fragrant flowers, each up to 5in (12.5cm) in diameter. Sepals and petals may be reddish, purplish or yellowish-brown inside and whitish on the back. The trumpet-shaped lip has a yellow throat and scarlet sides. Egg-shaped pseudobulbs are 1–3in (2.5–7.5cm) long; the leaves are 12–40in (30–100cm) long, lance shaped and folded.

ORIGIN China and Australia
TEMPERATURES Day 80–90°F (27–32°C), night 65–70°F (18–21°C)
LIGHT Bright filtered sun
BLOOMING PERIOD Winter and spring
CULTIVATION Pot in a mixture of equal parts aged cow manure, sandy loam and osmunda or peat moss, with lots of drainage crock in the bottom. Water generously but provide a cool, dry rest period to induce flowering. Divide and repot plants every two or three years after the blooming season.

PROMENAEA XANTHINA SUBFAMILY **VANDOIDEAE** TRIBE **MAXILLARIEAE**

Short stems rising from the bases of pseudobulbs bear 1 or 2 golden-yellow flowers with reddish-brown markings in the throat of the proportionally long lip. The blossoms are fragrant and long lasting. Pseudobulbs are oval, densely clustered, compressed and about 1in (2.5cm) tall, with a pair of 3in (7.5cm) oblong or lance-shaped leaves at the tip of each.

ORIGIN Brazil
TEMPERATURES Day 70–85°F (21–29°C), night 60–65°F (16–18°C)
LIGHT Filtered sun
BLOOMING PERIOD Summer
CULTIVATION This species does very well in a shallow pot or basket filled with a well-drained medium such as a mixture of equal parts osmunda fibre, finely chopped bark and sphagnum. Keep the medium moist during active growth but avoid getting water on newly formed shoots, which would cause rotting. Afterwards, provide a dry rest period of several weeks.

SOBRALIA MACRANTHA SUBFAMILY **EPIDENDROIDEAE** TRIBE **ARETHUSEAE**

The reed-like stems of this very large plant grow in thick, bushy clusters and may achieve a height of 7ft (2.1m). The leaves, well spaced along the stem's entire length, are 6–10in (15–25cm) long, lance shaped and leathery, with prominent veins. Very large flowers, up to 9in (22.5cm) in diameter, open one at a time atop the stems. They are a rich rose-purple with narrow, twisted sepals, broader wavy petals and a very large, intricately wrinkled lip, with a white throat enclosing several yellow ridges.

ORIGIN Mexico, Guatemala and Costa Rica
TEMPERATURES Day 65–75°F (18–24°C), night 55–60°F (13–16°C)
LIGHT Partial sun
BLOOMING PERIOD Spring and summer
CULTIVATION *S. macrantha* requires a very large pot and a rich, well-drained compost such as a mixture of loam, cow manure, osmunda fibre and leaf mould. Water copiously during active growth, then taper off, never allowing the roots to dry out completely. It requires abundant light and may be grown outdoors in subtropical climates.

65–75°F 18–24°C   55–60°F 13–16°C

THUNIA ALBA SUBFAMILY **EPIDENDROIDEAE** TRIBE **ARETHUSEAE**

Skinny, spindle-shaped pseudobulbs up to 40in (1m) tall are almost completely sheathed by the bases of alternate, leathery, oblong to lance-shaped leaves 6in (15cm) or less in length. The terminal inflorescence is somewhat pendulous and usually includes 5 to 10 white, satiny flowers 2–3in (5–7.5cm) in diameter. The funnel-shaped lips have a ruffled margin and pink or lavender veins.

ORIGIN Northern India and Burma
TEMPERATURES Day 65–75°F (18–24°C), night 55–60°F (13–16°C)
LIGHT Partial sun
BLOOMING PERIOD Late spring and summer
CULTIVATION Use a pot proportional to the plant's size. A well-drained compost of osmunda fibre, leaf-mould or a mixture of bark and sphagnum reportedly yield best results. Water copiously and frequently through the growth period until the flowers drop, then stop until new roots are several inches long. If necessary, repot during the dry rest period.

65–75°F 18–24°C
55–60°F 13–16°C

ZYGOPETALUM INTERMEDIUM SUBFAMILY **VANDOIDEAE** TRIBE **MAXILLARIEAE**

70–85°F
21–29°C

55–65°F
13–18°C

Stiff, erect inflorescences, usually about 2ft (60cm) tall, are composed of 5 to 8 showy, boldly marked flowers. The sweetly fragrant blooms are about 3in (7.5cm) in diameter with green sepals and petals splotched with reddish-brown and a spreading white lip streaked with magenta. They rise from 3in (7.5cm) pseudobulbs which are conical or egg shaped and have 3 to 5 elliptical or lance-shaped, leathery leaves, up to 2ft (60cm) long, originating at the tip.

ORIGIN Brazil, Peru and Bolivia

TEMPERATURES Day 70–85°F (21–29°C), night 55–65°F (13–18°C)

LIGHT Partial sun

BLOOMING PERIOD Autumn and winter

CULTIVATION Grow in medium to large pots with a medium consisting of one part potting soil to one part tree-fern fibre, leaf-mould, shredded osmunda, fine bark or sphagnum moss. Water and fertilize it regularly and abundantly throughout the year, allowing only a brief dry rest period after new growth matures. Provide the plant with good ventilation.

– BIBLIOGRAPHY –

Baker, Margaret L. and Charles O. Baker *Orchid Species Culture* (1991. Portland, Oregon).

Bechtel, Helmut, Phillip Cribb, and Edmund Launert *The Manual of Cultivated Orchid Species* (3rd ed. 1992. Dorset, UK).

Fanfani, Alberto and Walter Rossi *Simon & Schuster's Guide to Orchids* (1989. New York, NY).

Kramer, Jack *Orchids* (1970. Menlo Park, California).

Northen, Rebecca Tyson *Home Orchid Growing* (1990. New York, NY).

Tibbs, Mike and Ray Bilton *Orchids: An Illustrated Identifier and Guide to Cultivation* (1990. London, UK).

– ACKNOWLEDGEMENTS AND PICTURE CREDITS –

Credits listed by page number, t = top, b = bottom.

Harry Smith Collection: 19t, 19b, 22b, 23t, 25t, 26t, 30, 34t, 39t, 39b, 40b, 41, 42b, 43b, 45b, 48t, 49t, 52t, 52b, 54b, 56t, 56b, 57b, 59b, 61b, 63t, 65b, 70b, 72t, 74b, 76t, 76b, 77t.

Royal Botanic Gardens, Kew: 7, 23b, 24t, 27t, 29t, 29b, 31t, 31b, 34b, 36t, 38t, 42t, 47b, 48b, 49b, 51, 53t, 54t, 58, 60b, 61t, 62t, 63b, 64t, 64b, 65t, 66b, 67b, 68t, 68b, 69t, 69b, 70t, 72b, 73t, 75b.

Paul and Jenne Davies: 25b, 26b, 32t, 59t, 78.

David Menzies: 15, 20b, 21, 24b, 27b, 40t, 53b, 60t, 73b, 74t, 75t, 77b.

Joyce Stewart: 6, 8, 18t, 18b, 20t, 22t, 32b, 35, 36b, 38b, 43t, 44, 45t, 47t, 50t, 50b, 57t, 62b, 60t.

Quintet Publishing would like to extend special thanks to Dr Phillip Cribb at the Royal Botanic Gardens, Kew.

ALTERNATE: the arrangement of single leaves in which each leaf grows from a different node alternating on opposite sides of the stem.

ANTHER: the pollen-bearing portion of the stamen, the male reproductive structure.

APEX: the tip.

APICAL: at or pertaining to the tip.

AXIL: the angle between the upper surface of the leaf and the stem.

BASAL: at or pertaining to the base (usually of the stem or pseudobulb).

BILOBED: divided into two lobes.

BRACT: a specialized leaf, usually at the base of a flower or inflorescence.

CALLUS: the swollen portion of the lip.

COLUMN: the fused reproductive parts of a flower (stamens and pistil).

CROSS-POLLINATION: the pollination of a flower by one from a separate plant, ensuring genetic diversity within the species.

DECIDUOUS: describes a plant which sheds its leaves annually.

EPIPHYTE: a plant growing non-parasitically above the ground on another plant, log, or other structure.

FAMILY: a group of closely-related genera (or tribes, as in the orchid family).

GENUS: a group of related species.

HABITAT: the natural home of an organism.

HYBRID: the offspring produced when two different species of orchid are cross-pollinated.

INFLORESCENCE: a cluster of flowers sharing a common stalk.

LIP: the modified lower petal of an orchid flower.

LITHOPHYTE: a plant which grows on rocks.

MARGIN: the edge of a leaf, petal, or sepal.

MONOPODIAL: the growth pattern of orchids with only one main stem, which grows from a terminal bud.

NODE: a joint (usually with a leaf) on the stem.

OSMUNDA: the roots of the fern *Osmunda regalis*, a common growing medium used in orchid cultivation.

PENDULOUS: hanging downwards.

PERLITE: a water-retaining, soil-aerating or compost additive.

PETALS: the inner parts of the orchid flower, usually consisting of two petals that are identical and one, the lip, that is significantly modified.

POLLINIA: specialized pollen-containing pellets of orchids.

PSEUDOBULB: the swollen stem of an epiphytic orchid, usually as a reservoir for water.

RHIZOME: the modified, often underground, portion of the stem, which serves as a storage site for food and water.

SEPALS: the outer parts of a flower (three in orchids).

SPECIES: a group of organisms with one or more unique characteristics in common that set them apart from other organisms.

SPHAGNUM: moss of the genus *Sphagnum* used as a growing medium.

SYMPODIAL: the growth pattern of orchids with a creeping rhizome that gives rise to pseudobulbs.

TERMINAL: of or pertaining to the tip.

TERRESTRIAL: plants which are rooted in soil.

TREE-FERN FIBRE: a growing medium obtained from plants of the genus *Dicksonia*.

TRILOBED: having three lobes.

INDEX